# A FRENCH CHEF IN AMERICA

Every effort has been made to document and support all claims made by Jean Paul Combettes in writing the book A French Chef in America. However, in some cases it has been necessary to rely on his memory, and Jean Paul Combettes verifies that all claims made by him are true to the best of his knowledge and ability.

*Jean Paul Combettes*

# DEDICATION

This book is dedicated to the DLM Corporation, whose generous assistance made this project possible, and to Robert L. Mott, whose assistance in documenting the recipes was so critical. A very special thank-you goes out to my niece, Chantal Viboud Caravita of the British Broadcasting Corporation, and my nephew, Gerard Cavaignac, for their help and cooperation in researching and sending information from my home country of France.

I would also like to dedicate this book to my family: Marie, Muriel, Audrey, and my son, John, without whom there would be no story.

*Jean Paul Combettes*
*1991*

*Note:* The recipes in this book were reviewed and tested by Robert L. Mott, who apprenticed under Jean Paul from 1987 to 1988. He is a graduate of the California Culinary Academy and works as a chef in the Seattle area.

# Contents

# INTRODUCTION

*The way to get people involved with each other
is to involve them over food.*

Prince Maurice de Talleyrand Perigord,
Foreign Minister to Napoleon Bonaparte

Jean Paul Combettes was born in 1911 in Montpellier, France, on the Mediterranean Sea. His career as a chef was first inspired by his father, Albert, who opened a hotel and restaurant in Montpellier in 1897. Albert established his reputation with buffet-type meals for travelers and, later, with banquets, weddings, and catering. Jean Paul apprenticed under his father's supervision for three years, and several of the recipes included in this book are taken from Albert's menus.

In 1929 Jean Paul received an invitation to work with Chef Boucaire at the Meurice Hotel in Cannes, France. He left his father's employ for the first of many positions in leading hotels throughout Europe: the Hotel Majestic in Cannes, a renowned kitchen under Chef M. Louis Bonfillon (1935); the Hotel Metropole in Brighton, England, where Jean Paul assisted Chef Eugene Herbodeau and a team of 80 cooks in commemorating the 25th Jubilee celebration of King George V's reign (1936); and the Hotel Eden in Rome, Italy, a luxurious hotel where dethroned King Alfonso XIII of Spain and King Gustav of Sweden both stayed during Jean Paul's tenure (1937).

Jean Paul's exciting new career was interrupted by World War II, when he served in the French army, although during the war he also managed to operate a restaurant and movie theater in Saint Gilles. After the German occupation ended, he reopened his father's restaurant in Montpellier, which had been closed because of the fighting. (Interestingly, during World War I English troops occupied a portion of Pere Combettes' hotel; the property was thus renamed the Royal Hotel in their honor and still exists under that name today.) His energies were then relocated to Sète, France — an area popular for its production of the aperitif vermouth — where he became head chef at the Grand Hotel in 1945. An important hotel guest at this time was Prince Andargue Massai, son and heir of Haile Selassie, Emperor of Ethiopia. The Prince was so impressed with Jean Paul's abilities that he later

**The Royal Hotel,
Montpellier, France.**

wrote to him, offering him a three-year contract as executive chef for the Gondar Palace in Ethiopia. While in Sète, however, Jean Paul had met and married Marie Paule Pinsolle, and their young daughter was diagnosed as having a heart condition that could be treated only in the United States. He turned down the Prince's offer and in 1951 moved his family to Cleveland, Ohio.

Emile Burgermeister, a well-known chef living in the United States, convinced Jean Paul to make the move and was instrumental in getting his daughter admitted to the Cleveland Clinic, where she underwent two successful operations. Jean Paul, who was then 40 years old, had difficulty adjusting to America, the English language, and differing menu and cooking styles. Eventually, and with Emile's help, he was hired by the Zephyr Room, a nightclub in Cleveland, where he began again to achieve the success he had enjoyed in Europe, even appearing on several local television programs. From Cleveland, he moved in 1954 to the prestigious St. Francis Hotel in San Francisco and, in the same year, won a gold award in the seafood category at the International Culinary Exhibition. A year later, John Rickey, owner of several properties throughout the Bay area, hired Jean Paul as managing chef for Dinah's Shack, a popular old-time restaurant in Palo Alto. He held this position continuously for the next 16 years, becoming mentor to many American and European apprentices and building a reputation for his skills at banquets and receptions, just as his father did before him.

Although Jean Paul organized receptions for many impressive figures, such as Nobel Prize winner Dr. Robert Hofstadter and astronauts Neil Armstrong and Edwin ("Buzz") Aldrin, it was in the early 1970s, when he moved to the Sahara Hotel and Casino in Lake Tahoe, that he received the sobriquet, "Chef to the Stars." First as executive chef in an exclusive restaurant and then as personal chef for the Entertainers' Villa, Jean Paul served America's royalty — Hollywood entertainers! Performers he cooked for included Liberace, the Carpenters — Karen Carpenter sat in the kitchen and took notes on Jean Paul's recipes — Tom Jones, Tony Orlando, Dean Martin, Helen Reddy, the Jackson Five, Diana Ross, Frank Sinatra, and Sammy Davis, Jr. Twelve years after staying at the Sahara, Anne Murray remembered Jean Paul's food and company and invited him backstage at a concert in Seattle. Jean Paul lived up to his reputation and received many mementos from these stars.

Feeling a need for a less demanding lifestyle, however, Jean Paul and his family decided to move to Oak Harbor, Washington, in 1975 and enjoy a semiretirement. His older daughter had joined the Navy and was based on Whidbey Island, so he continued to supervise occasional banquets for area naval bases and give culinary demonstrations at nearby Skagit Valley College and at the local Y.M.C.A. Fortuitously, Jean Paul met Joe and Elisa

Franssen, owners of the Auld Holland Inn in Oak Harbor. They enlisted his help in developing the kitchen and menus for a new restaurant, Kasteel Franssen, that they opened in 1983. He also personally trained their son, Michael, in the traditional French methods, and Michael currently acts as one of the restaurant's managing chefs. The menus Jean Paul developed earned a triple diamond rating from the American Automobile Association (AAA) and took two first prizes at the 1988 Culinary Exhibitions in Bellingham, Washington. Today, Jean Paul continues to provide help and advice to the staff at Kasteel Franssen, demonstrating the same culinary skills and finesse that have given him such a successful and enriching career.

# APPETIZERS

*Hotel Courtes, 1914. Purchased by
Jean Paul's father, Albert Combettes
in Montpellier, France.*

# CHAMPIGNONS FARCIS

*Stuffed Mushrooms*

Preheat oven to 375°F. ♦ Clean mushrooms and remove stems. Finely chop stems and reserve for the stuffing. ♦ In a large skillet heat oil over medium heat, and lightly brown mushroom caps on top and bottom. Arrange top side down on a baking sheet. ♦ Add butter to the skillet and sauté shallots and mushroom stems. Continue cooking, stirring constantly, for about 2 minutes. Season with salt and pepper. ♦ Add Sauce Béchamel to the shallot-and-mushroom mixture and stir with a wooden or rubber spatula until combined. Allow mixture to cool slightly. ♦ Spoon filling into mushroom caps. Combine bread crumbs and Parmesan cheese and sprinkle liberally over stuffed mushroom caps. Bake on center rack of oven until tender and golden brown.

*Serves 6.*

**12 large mushrooms, each approximately 2 ½ inches in diameter**

**1 tablespoon vegetable oil**

**3 tablespoons butter**

**¼ cup diced shallots**

**1 teaspoon salt**

**½ teaspoon pepper**

**½ cup bread crumbs**

**½ cup grated Parmesan cheese**

**1 cup Sauce Béchamel (see page 107)**

# Champignons à L'Escargot

*Mushrooms with Snails*

In a small mixing bowl, combine butter, lemon juice, shallots, garlic, parsley, salt, and pepper until well mixed. Set aside in refrigerator. ♦ Preheat oven to 450°F. ♦ In a large skillet, heat oil over medium heat. Place mushroom caps top down in the skillet and sauté until lightly browned. Turn and sauté other side. ♦ Arrange caps on a baking sheet top side down. Place 1 snail in each cap and place a dollop of the butter mixture on top of each. Sprinkle with bread crumbs. Place baking sheet in the oven for approximately 2 minutes or until butter has melted and has begun to sizzle. Remove and serve.

*Helen Reddy once appeared on "The Tonight Show" and told Johnny Carson that Jean Paul was the only person who had convinced her to try snails. He prepared this dish for her, and after a tentative first bite, she promptly cleaned her plate.*

*Serves 6.*

**12 ounces butter, softened**

**2 tablespoons lemon juice**

**2 tablespoons chopped shallots**

**2 tablespoons minced garlic**

**⅓ cup chopped fresh parsley**

**1 teaspoon salt**

**½ teaspoon pepper**

**2 tablespoons oil**

**24 large mushroom caps, stems removed**

**2 dozen canned snails**

**3 tablespoons bread crumbs**

# Salmon Cured in Olive Oil

*D*ry salmon. Mix together salt, sugar, and dill. Rub the mixture into the fillets evenly over all. ♦ Place fillets flat in a shallow pan, cover with waxed paper and place another pan on top. Weight the pan on top with several heavy cans, applying pressure to the fillets. Place in the refrigerator for at least 24 hours. ♦ Remove salmon from pan, dry it well with paper towels and, with a fish filleting knife, slice the salmon very thin, about ¼ inch thick. ♦ Pack salmon slices into preserve jars, squeezing firmly. Fill the jars with olive oil and cover tightly with lids. Keep in refrigerator for at least 48 hours before serving. ♦ Arrange slices on a platter and garnish with lemon slices, raw onion rings, and capers, or serve on pumpernickel bread. Salmon may also be broiled or barbecued quickly, about 1 minute on each side.

*Jean Paul often catered parties for the naval officers on Whidbey Island, Washington; this Northwest specialty was a popular request.*

*Serves 8–10*

**3 pounds fresh salmon fillet, skinned**

**4 tablespoons salt**

**2 tablespoons sugar**

**1 tablespoon fresh dill or ½ teaspoon dried dill**

**1 cup olive oil (or enough to cover salmon in each of the jars)**

**10 half-pint preserve jars**

# Moules Mayonnaise

*Mussels with Mayonnaise*

Place mussels in a saucepan with Chablis, peppercorns, thyme, and bay leaf. Cover pan and simmer, stirring occasionally by lifting the mussels from the bottom to the top. Steam until mussels are opened. Discard any that remain closed; this is an indication that they were not fresh when preparation began. Drain mussels; cool, remove meat from the shells, and set aside. You may want to save half of each shell to place the mussels in for serving. ♦ In a mixing bowl combine mayonnaise with Dijon mustard, lemon juice, and Worcestershire sauce. ♦ Transfer mussels to a serving platter or to the half shells, spoon sauce over each one, and serve.

*Serves 6.*

2 quarts mussels, scrubbed and debearded

½ cup Chablis

1 teaspoon peppercorns

Pinch of thyme

1 bay leaf

1 cup mayonnaise

1 tablespoon Dijon mustard

1 teaspoon lemon juice

1 teaspoon Worcestershire sauce

# Huîtres à la Jean Paul

*Oysters Jean Paul*

Open oysters and keep them in the deeper half of each shell, making sure there are no shell fragments inside. In 3 to 5 cake pans, pour rock salt to a depth of 1 inch. Distribute and set oysters in each pan. Pour a small amount of vermouth over each oyster. ♦ Preheat oven to 450°F. ♦ Cream together butter, shallots, garlic, parsley, salt, and pepper in a bowl. ♦ Place a dollop of butter mixture on each oyster and sprinkle with bread crumbs. Place pans in the upper third of the oven and bake 5 minutes or until butter sizzles. Place pans on a serving dish and serve immediately. ♦ Accompany with garlic bread on the side.

*Serves 6.*

**36 oysters in their shells**

**1 bag rock salt**

**1 cup dry vermouth**

**12 ounces butter, softened**

**4 tablespoons chopped shallots**

**3 tablespoons chopped garlic**

**½ cup chopped fresh parsley**

**1 teaspoon salt**

**½ teaspoon black pepper**

**½ cup bread crumbs**

# Écrivisses à la Nage

*Crayfish in Court Bouillon*

Soak crayfish in milk for at least 3 hours before preparation. ♦ Place rest of the ingredients in a stockpot and bring to a boil. Allow the court bouillon to simmer for 10 minutes. ♦ Remove crayfish from milk and plunge them into the court bouillon. Cook at a rolling boil for about 8 minutes. ♦ Remove crayfish from court bouillon and place in serving bowls. Reduce poaching liquid by half, strain through a sieve, and pour over the crayfish. Serve warm or cold. ♦ Present the crayfish draped over the edge of a cocktail dish, with the court bouillon in the bowl portion. Use as a first course in a formal dinner.

*Jean Paul created this dish while at a 15th century castle-turned-hotel, the Chateau de la Caze on the Tarn River in France (1931). Below the kitchen was a storage area built next to the river's edge, so crayfish and trout could be submerged in the river in wire enclosures, ensuring absolute freshness for this and other recipes.*

*Serves 6.*

**48 live crayfish**

**1 quart milk**

**2 medium carrots, sliced**

**2 medium onions, sliced**

**1 teaspoon dried thyme**

**1 bay leaf**

**1 rib celery, sliced**

**1 tablespoon salt**

**1 teaspoon peppercorn**

**3 cups Chablis wine**

**3 cups water**

# Bouchée au Crabe

*Crab in Pastry Shell*

Bake pastry shells as directed on package. ♦ Sauté onion in saucepan with butter or oil over medium heat. When onion is translucent, add thyme and bay leaf. Combine flour and curry powder and sprinkle over onion. Mix well and add stock. Bring to a simmer over medium heat, and cook for 30 minutes. Stir in heavy cream until combined. ♦ Combine 2 cups of the sauce with the cooked crab and heat briefly. Fill pastry shells with mixture and serve immediately with extra sauce on the side. ♦ Sauce Mornay may be used in place of Curry Sauce.

*Serves 6.*

1 package of 6 prepared individual puff pastry shells

½ pound cooked crab

**CURRY SAUCE:**

1 onion, diced very finely

1 tablespoon butter or ¾ tablespoon olive oil

1 teaspoon thyme

1 bay leaf

3 tablespoons flour

1½ teaspoons curry powder

3½ cups white stock

4 tablespoons heavy cream

# Canapés Aveyronais

*Blue Cheese Spread*

Combine blue cheese, butter, Worcestershire sauce, and cayenne in a bowl and mash well with a fork. Cover and refrigerate. Spread mixture on crackers or use as a stuffing for celery.

*Yields 1 cup.*

**8 ounces blue cheese, crumbled**

**4 ounces butter, softened**

**½ teaspoon Worcestershire sauce**

**Dash cayenne**

**Crackers or celery ribs**

# FOIES DE CANARD EN TERRINE

*Pâté of Duck Livers*

Preheat oven to 350°F. ♦ Wash livers in cold water and place in a skillet. Cover with water, heat until close to boiling and cool immediately under cold running water. ♦ Drain livers and dice in a meat grinder or food processor. ♦ Chop ham and bacon. Add egg yolks, salt, pepper, paprika, nutmeg, basil, and Cognac. Mix well, add chopped livers, and mix well again. ♦ Transfer ingredients to an ovenproof paté mold or terrine, cover the top with foil, and seal well. ♦ Place the terrine in a roasting pan and add water to come one-third of the way up the side of the terrine. Bake for about 1 hour. The paté is done when the fat at the surface is clear and the center temperature reaches 175°F. ♦ Remove from oven and let paté cool completely in the terrine. Clean the outside of the terrine and present on a folded cloth napkin placed on a long platter. Slice at the table.

*Serves 10.*

**2 pounds duck livers**

**1½ pounds cooked ham, finely chopped**

**1 pound fresh (unsmoked) bacon**

**3 egg yolks**

**1 tablespoon salt**

**1 teaspoon pepper**

**½ teaspoon paprika**

**Pinch of nutmeg**

**1 teaspoon chopped fresh basil**

**3 tablespoons Cognac**

# Pâté de Foie de Volaille

*Chicken Liver Pâté*

Hard-boil eggs, remove shells, and chop eggs. Set aside. ♦ Melt butter in skillet over medium-high heat. Add chicken livers and brown well on all sides. Add shallots and continue cooking and stirring 1 more minute. Remove from heat and allow mixture to cool slightly. ♦ In a food processor, mix together livers and eggs. Add cream cheese, brandy, salt, pepper, and paprika; continue mixing until combined. Transfer mixture to an airtight container and refrigerate. Use as a spread with crackers.

*Serves 10 to 12.*

**3 eggs**

**3 tablespoons butter**

**2 pounds chicken livers**

**2 teaspoons chopped shallots**

**10 ounces cream cheese, softened**

**3 tablespoons brandy**

**1½ teaspoons salt**

**1 teaspoon pepper**

**1 teaspoon paprika**

# TERRINE DE PÂTÉ MAISON

*Pâté Home Style*

Preheat oven to 400°F. ♦ Wash chicken livers in cold water and drain. Place in a bowl and marinate with the 2 tablespoons of brandy, salt, and pepper while you prepare the rest of the ingredients. ♦ Blanch bacon slices in boiling water for 1 minute. Remove and drain. ♦ Combine all ground meats and ground fat in a large mixing bowl. Add shallots, garlic, salt, pepper, paprika, eggs, and the ⅓ cup of Cognac or brandy. Mix with a wooden spoon or your hands until well blended. ♦ Line a 4- by 8-inch earthenware loaf pan or terrine with the bacon slices. Spoon half the meat mixture into the bacon-lined mold, pressing down slightly to remove any air pockets. Arrange chicken livers down the middle of the pan. Spoon the remaining meat mixture over the chicken livers and smooth the top, pressing lightly again. Fold ends of bacon slices over the top of the mold and press down slightly in order to keep in place. ♦ Cover mold with aluminum foil, making sure the edges are well sealed. Place the mold in a roasting pan, and pour water into the pan until water level is halfway up the side of the mold. Place the roasting pan in the bottom one-third of the oven and bake for 1½ to 2 hours. Check with a thermometer for doneness; the terrine is ready to be removed from the oven when the temperature in the center reaches 175°F. Remove mold from the water bath and allow to cool to room temperature; then remove foil. Refrigerate until ready to serve. Slice ⅓ inch thick and garnish with fresh parsley.

*Jean Paul developed this recipe during the winter of 1931, when he assisted in the making and canning of pâtés at the Hotel Berthier in Espalion, France. The terrine should be sliced one-third of the way back and presented on a long platter with a parsley and sliced lemon border.*

*Serves 10.*

1 pound whole chicken livers

2 tablespoons brandy

1 teaspoon salt

½ teaspoon pepper

8 slices bacon

1½ pounds lean pork, ground

1 pound fresh pork fat, ground

1 pound lean ground veal or ground turkey

3 shallots, chopped

4 cloves garlic, minced

4 teaspoons salt

4 teaspoons ground pepper

2 eggs, slightly beaten

⅓ cup Cognac or brandy

3 teaspoons paprika

Fresh parsley sprigs, for garnish

# Soups & Salads

*Photo of Jean Paul Combettes,*
*1913, at the age of 2½*
*Montpellier, France.*

# Soupe à L'Oignon Gratinée

*French Onion Soup au Gratin*

In a 4-quart soup kettle, melt the 2 ounces of butter with the oil. Add onions and cook uncovered over medium heat, stirring often with a wooden spoon, until onions are light brown. Add flour and cook, stirring, for about 1 minute. ♦ Pour in beef bouillon; add salt, pepper, thyme, bay leaf, and garlic. Cover pot and simmer over medium heat for 30 minutes. ♦ Arrange sliced French bread in a pan and toast in a 300°F. oven until the slices are dry and lightly brown. ♦ Ladle soup into ovenproof serving bowls, place 2 slices toasted French bread in each, spread grated Swiss and Parmesan over bread, and sprinkle 1 teaspoon melted butter over each bowl. Place bowls under broiler until cheese is melted and top is lightly browned. Serve immediately.

*Serves 6.*

**2 ounces butter**

**3 tablespoons vegetable oil**

**2 pounds onions, thinly sliced (any variety except red)**

**4 tablespoons flour**

**2 quarts beef bouillon or 4 11-ounce cans beef consommé**

**Salt and pepper to taste**

**½ teaspoon thyme**

**1 small bay leaf**

**3 cloves garlic, minced**

**12 slices French bread, ⅔ inch thick**

**1 cup grated Swiss cheese**

**½ cup grated Parmesan cheese**

**2 tablespoons melted butter**

# Crème Boula-Boula

*Cream Boula-Boula*

Cook peas in salted water for 12 minutes or until tender. Drain well, place in a blender, and pureé. Transfer to a medium-sized saucepan. ♦ Over low heat, whisk in beef bouillon until smooth. Increase heat to medium and bring pureé to a simmer while stirring in butter. Add sherry and season with salt and pepper. Simmer, stirring continuously to prevent scorching, until thick. ♦ Whip cream until slightly thick but not stiff. Pour soup into individual ovenproof bowls and garnish each with 1 tablespoon whipped cream. Place under broiler for approximately 1 minute or until cream is slightly browned on top. Remove from oven and serve.

*This cream soup was the creation of Chef Magrin of the* Normandie, *the largest and most luxurious ocean liner that crossed the Atlantic before World War II. Magrin was from Pézenas, France, a town near Montpellier, and was friends with Albert Combettes.*

*Serves 6.*

**3 cups fresh green peas, shelled**

**1 12-ounce can condensed beef bouillon**

**2 tablespoons butter**

**½ cup sherry**

**1 teaspoon salt**

**½ teaspoon pepper**

**1 cup heavy cream**

# SOUPE VICHYSSOISE

*Cream Vichyssoise*

Cook potatoes in boiling salted water until very tender. Drain and set aside.♦ In a medium-sized skillet, melt butter over medium heat and sauté leek until tender. ♦ Place potatoes, salt, pepper, cayenne pepper, leek, and chicken bouillon in an electric blender or food processor. Cover and blend on high speed for 10 seconds. Add cream and blend on medium speed for 10 more seconds. ♦ Chill soup in refrigerator for at least 2 hours before serving. Mix in chives and Worcestershire sauce, ladle into serving bowls, garnish with whole chives, and serve.

*Serves 6.*

**3 medium potatoes, peeled and cut in half**

**1 4-ounce stick butter**

**1 whole leek (green and white), chopped**

**1 tablespoon salt**

**1 teaspoon pepper**

**½ teaspoon cayenne pepper**

**2 cups chicken bouillon**

**1 cup heavy cream**

**2 teaspoons chopped chives**

**1 teaspoon Worcestershire sauce**

**Whole chives, for garnish**

# Soupe Gazpacho

*Gazpacho*

Dice very finely the green peppers, cucumbers, onions, radishes, and tomatoes. ♦ Place diced vegetables in a large bowl, add garlic, and season with salt, pepper, cayenne, and dill. While stirring briskly, gradually add olive oil, consommé, cold water, and Worcestershire sauce. Chill in refrigerator for at least 30 minutes. Adjust seasonings and serve in individual chilled soup bowls.

*Gazpacho is very popular in Spain, particularly in Andalusia, where the climate becomes quite hot during summer months. It is usually served at lunch.*

*Serves 6.*

**4 green peppers, seeded**

**2 cucumbers, peeled and seeded**

**2 large onions**

**8 radishes**

**4 large ripe tomatoes**

**3 cloves garlic, minced**

**1½ teaspoons salt**

**½ tablespoon pepper**

**½ teaspoon cayenne pepper**

**2 tablespoons fresh dill, chopped**

**¼ cup olive oil**

**2 12-ounce cans beef consommé**

**3 cups cold water**

**1 tablespoon Worcestershire sauce**

# Potage Crème de Champignons

*Cream of Mushroom Soup*

In a 4-quart soup kettle, melt butter and oil over medium heat. Add mushrooms and shallots. Sauté 5 minutes, stirring occasionally, until mushrooms are tender. Sprinkle flour over mushrooms and mix to form a paste. Add chicken bouillon and whisk soup until well mixed. Simmer for 10 minutes over medium heat, stirring occasionally to prevent scorching. Season with salt, pepper, and cayenne; add heavy cream. Stir well until combined. Serve.

*Serves 6.*

**1 4-ounce stick butter**

**2 tablespoons vegetable oil**

**1½ pounds fresh mushrooms, finely diced**

**3 shallots, finely diced**

**6 tablespoons flour**

**3 12-ounce cans chicken bouillon**

**2 teaspoons salt**

**1 teaspoon white pepper**

**⅛ teaspoon cayenne pepper**

**1 cup heavy cream**

# Purée de Pois Cassés

*Split Pea Soup*

Soak peas in water for 1 hour. ♦ In a heavy 4-quart kettle, cook ham hock in water for about 5 minutes. Remove hock, empty kettle, and add 3 quarts of fresh water. Place ham hock back in kettle and simmer for at least 1 more hour. ♦ Add soaked peas and continue simmering 10 minutes. In a sauté pan, sauté leek, onion, and celery in butter and oil until tender. Add sautéed vegetables and thyme to the soup kettle and simmer for 1½ hours. ♦ Remove ham hock, purée soup in a blender or food processor, and put back into kettle. ♦ Dice meat from ham hock and add to soup. Slice frankfurters about ¼ inch thick and add. Simmer another 10 minutes, season to taste with salt and pepper, and add butter. ♦ Ladle soup into individual soup bowls and serve.

*Serves 6.*

2 cups green split peas

1 smoked ham hock

1 large leek, chopped (both white and green parts)

1 cup finely chopped onions

1 cup finely chopped celery

3 tablespoons butter

2 tablespoons vegetable oil

Pinch of thyme

2 frankfurters (optional)

Salt

Pepper

1 tablespoon butter

# Manhattan Clam Chowder

*I*n a 4-quart soup kettle, heat oil over medium heat. Add salt pork or bacon, leeks, onion, and celery; stir continuously and cook until onions and leeks are tender but not browned. ♦ Add the 2 pints clam juice plus the juice from the canned clams; bring to a boil over medium heat. Add potatoes and season with salt, pepper, garlic, bay leaf, thyme, and basil. Cover and continue cooking until potatoes are tender. Add tomatoes and clams and cook for 2 more minutes. Do not overcook the clams or they will become tough. Serve.

*Jean Paul's version of Manhattan Clam Chowder won first prize in 1987 at the West Coast Chowder Challenge in Bellingham, Washington.*

*Serves 6.*

**2 tablespoons olive oil**

**1 6-ounce slab salt pork or bacon, diced**

**2 leeks, chopped**

**1 large onion, chopped**

**3 8-ounce cans clams**

**2 ribs celery, chopped**

**2 pints clam juice**

**5 medium potatoes, diced**

**1 tablespoon salt**

**1 teaspoon pepper**

**4 cloves garlic, minced**

**1 bay leaf**

**1 teaspoon thyme**

**1 teaspoon basil**

**2 tomatoes, peeled, seeded, and chopped**

# Salade Niçoise

*Salad Niçoise*

Boil eggs in water until hard. Remove shells and cut eggs in quarters. ♦ Remove ends of green beans, removing strings if necessary. Cut into uniform 2-inch lengths. Bring to a boil 2 quarts of water with 1 teaspoon salt added. Add beans and cook until tender but not soft, about 12 minutes. Drain well. ♦ Place potatoes in a large saucepan and add enough water to cover. Add the remaining teaspoon of salt, bring to a boil, and cook until easily pierced with a fork. Run under cold water and, before completely cooled, peel potatoes and dice into 1-inch cubes. ♦ Cut tomatoes into wedges and set aside. ♦ Remove outer leaves of lettuce. Wash in cold water and drain well. Tear leaves and line a large salad bowl. Place diced potatoes in center of bowl. Arrange green beans, tomato wedges, quartered eggs, anchovy fillets, and olives all around the bowl. Ladle dressing over salad. Present salad to table and then toss and serve.

*Serves 6.*

**3 eggs**

**½ pound green beans**

**2 teaspoons salt, divided**

**4 medium potatoes**

**3 ripe, firm tomatoes**

**1 head Boston or butter lettuce**

**6 anchovy fillets**

**24 ripe olives**

**¾ cup Jean Paul Vinaigrette Dressing (see page 117)**

# Salade Caesar

*Caesar Salad*

The preparation of this salad should be done in front of your guests. Prepare a tray with all of your ingredients beforehand. ♦ Trim off and discard any discolored outer leaves of romaine and any discolored portions at the top. Cut romaine into 1½- to 2-inch squares. Wash well, drain, and chill in refrigerator. ♦ To prepare croutons: Melt butter in a sauté pan over low heat. Add bread cubes and half of the minced garlic. Sauté until edges of croutons turn golden brown. ♦ In a large wooden salad bowl, combine anchovies, mustard, egg yolk, lemon juice, salt, pepper, and remaining garlic. Mix well with a fork and stir in olive oil. ♦ Add lettuce and toss in dressing until well coated. Add croutons and sprinkle with Parmesan cheese. Toss again lightly and serve.

*Serves 6.*

**2 heads romaine lettuce**

**1 4-ounce stick butter**

**4 slices stale bread, diced**

**4 cloves garlic, minced**

**5 anchovy fillets, chopped (optional)**

**1 tablespoon Dijon mustard**

**1 egg yolk**

**3 tablespoons lemon juice**

**Salt and freshly ground pepper to taste**

**⅔ cup olive oil**

**½ cup grated Parmesan cheese**

# Salade de Pommes de Terre Nîmoise

*Potato Salad Nimoise*

Boil eggs in water until hard. Remove shells and chop eggs. Set aside. ♦ Place potatoes in a large saucepan and add enough water to cover. Add salt, bring to a boil, and cook until easily pierced with a fork. Run under cold water and, before completely cooled, peel potatoes and dice into 1-inch cubes. Cover and put in refrigerator to chill. ♦ Combine Jean Paul Vinaigrette Dressing and mayonnaise until well mixed. In a large bowl toss potatoes, green onions, chopped eggs, and celery with dressing until well coated. ♦ For presentation, arrange slices of green pepper around the edges of a serving bowl. Carefully place tossed salad in center of bowl; sprinkle with chopped parsley. Garnish with anchovy fillets and tomato rose. Serve.

*Serves 6.*

**3 eggs**

**3 pounds medium potatoes**

**1 teaspoon salt**

**1 cup Jean Paul Vinaigrette Dressing (see page 117)**

**2 tablespoons mayonnaise**

**½ cup chopped green onions**

**½ cup thinly sliced celery**

**2 green peppers, sliced**

**1 tablespoon chopped parsley**

**6 anchovy fillets**

**Tomato rose**

# SALADE DE HARICOTS VERTS

*Green Bean Salad*

Cook string beans in salted boiling water for 12 minutes or until tender but firm. Cool immediately under cold running water. ♦ Drain beans in a colander, place in a salad bowl, and pour dressing over them. Toss well. Arrange onion rings and tomato wedges over the top and serve.

*Serves 4.*

**1 pound fresh green beans**

**2 quarts water**

**1 tablespoon salt**

**½ cup Jean Paul Vinaigrette Dressing (see page 117)**

**1 Bermuda onion, cut in rings**

**1 large tomato, cut in wedges**

# COUSCOUS SALAD

*P*lace contents of Couscous Salad Mix in a bowl and stir in water, olive oil and lemon juice. Mix well and refrigerate for 10 minutes, or until water is completely absorbed. ♦ Add to the bowl the diced tomato, cucumber, parsley, and garlic. Mix well and return to refrigerator for another 15 minutes. ♦ Arrange lettuce leaves on a serving platter, turn the salad over the lettuce leaves, surround the platter with olives interspersed with tomato wedges, and serve.

*Serves 6.*

1 5- or 6-ounce package **Couscous Salad Mix (or bulgur wheat)**

1 cup cold water

⅓ cup olive oil

Juice of 1 lemon

1 large tomato (about ½ pound), peeled, seeded, and finely diced

1 medium cucumber, peeled, seeded and thinly sliced

3 sprigs parsley, chopped

2 cloves garlic, minced

Lettuce leaves

1 small can whole, pitted black olives, well drained

1 medium tomato, cut into wedges

# Asperges Vinaigrette

*Asparagus Vinaigrette*

Wash asparagus spears in cold water. Cut off bottom ends, making all spears uniform in length. Peel. Immerse in boiling salted water for about 10 minutes or until asparagus is easily pierced with a fork. ♦ Place pot under cold running water to stop the cooking process. Drain asparagus on a towel, arrange on a plate, and serve with Jean Paul Vinaigrette Dressing. Serve by sprinkling chopped hard-boiled eggs over the dressing and garnishing with a tomato rose and parsley.

*Serves 4.*

*1 pound asparagus*

*2 quarts water*

*1 tablespoon salt*

*½ cup Jean Paul Vinaigrette (see page 117)*

*2 eggs, hard-boiled*

# ENDIVES DE BELGIQUE

*Belgian Endive Salad*

*P*eel off the outer leaves of Belgian endive and wash in cold water. Dry well with a towel and chill in refrigerator. Slice leaves coarsely crosswise and place in a salad bowl. Toss with Jean Paul Vinaigrette Dressing just before serving. Add chopped hard-boiled eggs to the dressing or sprinkle over the salad.

*Serves 4.*

**1 head Belgian endive**

**½ cup Jean Paul Vinaigrette (see page 117)**

**2 eggs, hard-boiled**

# Meat

*"Mas De Lacombe", the country house*
*where Jean Paul vacationed with his*
*mother, Leontine Combettes.*

# Cassoulet du Languedoc

*Meat and White Bean Stew*

Preheat oven to 425°F. ♦ Place beans, water, carrots, celery, the 1 tablespoon plus 2 teaspoons of salt, and the pork shank in a large saucepan. Bring to a boil, cover, and simmer for about 1½ hours or until tender. ♦ While beans are cooking, place duck and pork shoulder in a roasting pan. Sprinkle with salt and pepper, also seasoning the duck cavity with salt and pepper, about ⅓ teaspoon of each. With a sharp knife, pierce four or five holes in pork and push in garlic cloves. Roast, uncovered, until browned. ♦ Reduce oven temperature to 375°F. Boil sausages in a pot for about 5 minutes or until they begin to swell. Arrange in a roasting pan, place in oven, and cook until brown. ♦ Remove beans from pot and place in an 8-quart ovenproof casserole dish. Meanwhile, remove duck and pork from oven, remove them from the pan, and set aside. Drain fat from the roasting pan and set aside. Add 1 cup water to roasting pan and deglaze on top of stove, scraping with a spoon to dissolve the browned juices, and pour over beans. Cut duck into eight pieces, slice roasted pork and sausage, and add to beans. ♦ Pour 2 tablespoons reserved duck and pork fat into a skillet. Place over medium heat, add onions, and sauté onions until they become transparent. Add minced garlic and tomato sauce. Continue cooking for another 5 minutes, then pour into bean mixture. ♦ Mix bread crumbs and parsley, and spread in a thick layer over cassoulet. Sprinkle with 3 or 4 tablespoons of fat to moisten, then place dish in middle of oven and bake for about 30 minutes at 350°F until nicely browned. ♦ Serve directly from the dish.

*This is a famous stew of white beans, sausage, poultry, and meat created in the French province of Languedoc, although argument arises over whether it originated in Toulouse, Castelnaudary, or Carcassonne. Disagreement also arises over the method of preparation and over the ingredients — duck or goose, pork or lamb. In fact, the dish probably originated with the Romans, who were established in the Provence, Languedoc, and Roussillon regions for centuries.*

*Serves 6 to 8.*

**4 cups small white beans, soaked no more than 2 hours**

**3 quarts water**

**2 large carrots, coarsely chopped**

**2 celery ribs, coarsely chopped**

**1 tablespoon plus 2 teaspoons salt**

**1 small pork shank**

**1 4-pound duck**

**4 pounds pork shoulder**

**1 teaspoon pepper**

**4 cloves garlic, whole**

**2 pounds sausage (Italian or Polish)**

**2 tablespoons fat from the roasted duck and pork**

**2 medium onions, chopped**

**4 cloves garlic, minced**

**1 8-ounce can tomato sauce**

**1½ cups fine dry bread crumbs**

**¼ cup fresh chopped parsley**

**3 to 4 tablespoons fat from the roasted duck and pork**

# Grenadin de Veau La Rotonde

*Veal Scallops La Rotonde*

Lightly season cutlets with salt, pepper, and paprika. Whisk together Madeira and olive oil and marinate cutlets for at least 1 hour. ♦ Remove cutlets, reserving marinade, and dry them slightly between two paper towels. In a large sauté pan, melt butter over medium heat and cook cutlets on each side until golden brown. Arrange cutlets on a serving platter and keep warm. ♦ Place pan back on heat, adding more oil or butter if necessary. Sauté mushrooms 1 minute or until tender. Add marinade and reduce to ⅓ cup. Stir in cream, and reduce further until sauce is thick enough to coat cutlets. Mix in lemon juice, spoon mushrooms and sauce over cutlets, and serve.

*"La Rotonde" was added to the names of many dishes Jean Paul created while at the Grand Hotel. This veal recipe was one of the restaurant's specialties.*

*Serves 6.*

**6 5-ounce veal cutlets (ask your butcher to cut them from the loin)**

**1 teaspoon salt**

**½ teaspoon pepper**

**Paprika**

**1 cup Madeira**

**5 tablespoons olive oil**

**2 tablespoons butter**

**2 cups fresh mushrooms, sliced**

**1 cup heavy cream**

**Juice of half a lemon**

# Veal Cutlets á la Sètoise

*Veal Cutlets Sète Style*

Marinate cutlets in Madeira and olive oil for 1 hour. Drain, reserving marinade. ♦ Season cutlets with salt, pepper, and paprika. In a medium-sized skillet over medium-high heat, heat butter or oil and sauté cutlets until browned on both sides. Remove from skillet and place on serving dish; keep warm. ♦ Sauté mushrooms in the same skillet over medium heat until tender. Pour in marinade and reduce by half. Add heavy cream and continue to reduce until thickened. Pour sauce over cutlets and serve.

*Jean Paul was chef at the Grand Hotel from 1946 to 1950. Located in the Mediterranean harbor of Sète, France — production capital for Taillan, Noilly Prat, and Martini & Rossi vermouths — it is an old, aristocratic resort and was often host to dinner meetings for the area's aperitif producers. This recipe is typical of what Jean Paul would serve.*

*Serves 6.*

**6 5-ounce veal cutlets, cut from the loin**

**1 cup Madeira**

**4 tablespoons olive oil**

**2 teaspoons salt**

**1 teaspoon pepper**

**1 teaspoon paprika**

**2 tablespoons butter or olive oil**

**1 cup sliced fresh mushrooms**

**1 cup fresh heavy cream**

# Carré de Veau Rôti Bouquetière à la Jean Paul

*Roast Veal Jean Paul Style Bouquetière*

Preheat oven to 450°F. ♦ Place veal and shallots in a roasting pan, season with salt and pepper, and roast for about 35 minutes or until browned all over. ♦ Reduce oven temperature to 350°F and cook for at least 1 more hour. To determine doneness, insert a meat thermometer into center of roast. The roast will be medium done when the temperature reaches 160°F. ♦ Transfer roast to a serving platter and keep warm. Place roasting pan over medium-high heat and pour in the cup dry white wine and the water. Bring to a boil while scraping the brown drippings from the bottom of the pan. Knead 2 tablespoons of the butter with the flour to make a *beurre manie*, and swirl into the gravy to thicken it slightly. ♦ Separately cook carrots, green beans, peas, artichoke hearts, and potatoes. While cooking carrots, add garlic and 2 tablespoons of butter. ♦ Sprinkle bread crumbs and Parmesan cheese over roast veal, and replace in oven for a few minutes. Arrange vegetables around roast on the platter "in bouquetière," each separate. Pour gravy over and serve.

*One of Jean Paul's favorite guests while at the Sahara was Liberace. This dish and Champignons au Crabe were among the pianist's favorites.*

*Serves 6.*

**1 5-pound veal rib roast (5 ribs, both sides of backbone, trimmed)**

**4 whole shallots**

**1 teaspoon salt**

**½ teaspoon pepper**

**½ cup Chablis or other dry white wine**

**½ cup water**

**4 tablespoons butter, divided**

**2 tablespoons flour**

**1 pound small Belgian carrots**

**1 pound green beans**

**2 cups shelled green peas**

**6 to 8 artichoke hearts**

**2 pounds red potatoes, peeled and quartered**

**1 clove garlic, chopped**

**½ cup dry bread crumbs**

**2 tablespoons grated Parmesan cheese**

# Escalopes de Veau Lozerienne

*Veal Scallops Lozerienne*

Season cutlets with salt and pepper and dredge lightly in flour. ♦ Dip cutlets into beaten egg and dredge in bread crumbs. ♦ Heat clarified butter in a large skillet over medium heat. Cook cutlets two at a time, searing until golden brown on each side. Place cutlets on a large oval platter and keep warm. ♦ Place in the center of each of the cutlets a round slice of lemon and a few capers. Cut the hard-boiled eggs lengthwise and carefully separate the yolks from the whites; rinse whites in water, being sure to remove all traces of yolk. Chop both the yolks and whites very finely, keeping them separate. Arrange remaining lemon slices down each side of platter and place piles of chopped yolks and whites decoratively at each end, separated by narrow strips of chopped parsley. Sprinkle rest of capers next to cutlets. ♦ Pour lemon juice and *beurre noisette* over veal. Serve.

*Doc Severinsen loved Italian food, and this dish, as well as Gnocchi à la Parisienne, was one of his favorites.*

*Serves 6.*

6 6-ounce veal cutlets sliced ¼ inch thick

1 teaspoon salt

½ teaspoon pepper

Flour (for dredging)

3 eggs, beaten

1 cup bread crumbs (for dredging)

3 tablespoons clarified butter

2 lemons, 1 sliced in rounds

½ cup capers

3 hard-boiled eggs

4 tablespoons chopped fresh parsley

Juice of 1 lemon

2 to 3 tablespoons beurre noisette (browned butter)

# Osso Bucco Milanaise

*Veal Shank Stew Milan Style*

$\mathcal{P}$reheat oven to 375°F. ♦ Heat olive oil in a large, thick-bottomed skillet over medium heat. Season veal shanks with salt and pepper; dredge in flour. Lightly brown all sides in the oil. Remove shanks and set aside. ♦ Add onion, carrots, celery, and garlic to the skillet. Cook over medium heat 5 minutes or until vegetables are slightly browned. Put shanks back into skillet, add mushrooms and tomatoes, and season with thyme and basil. Cook for 1 more minute; add wine and enough water to just cover shanks. ♦ Cover skillet, place in oven, and bake for 1½ hours. Add grated lemon rind and cook for 5 more minutes. Remove shanks to individual serving dishes and spoon a portion of the sauce over the top of each serving.

*Serves 6.*

⅓ cup olive oil

**2 veal shanks (ask your butcher to cut each into three pieces)**

**1½ teaspoons salt**

**½ teaspoon pepper**

**½ cup flour**

**1 large onion, finely chopped**

**1 cup diced carrots**

**1 rib celery, chopped**

**3 cloves garlic, minced**

**1 cup sliced mushrooms**

**2 large tomatoes, peeled, seeded, and chopped**

**1 teaspoon thyme**

**1 teaspoon basil**

**2 cups dry white wine**

**Rind of 1 lemon, grated**

# Cotes de Veau à la Crème aux Champignons

*Veal Chops Sautéed in Cream and Mushrooms*

Season cutlets with salt and pepper and lightly flour each side. Heat butter or olive oil in a heavy-bottomed skillet over medium-high heat. Cook cutlets on each side until lightly browned. Remove from skillet and place on a serving plate; keep warm. ♦ In the same skillet sauté mushrooms until slightly browned and tender, adding more butter or oil if necessary. Add heavy cream and a few drops of lemon juice. Continue to simmer until sauce is thick. ♦ Spoon sauce over cutlets and serve. ♦ Often served with buttered fettuccine.

*Serves 6.*

6 ¼-inch-thick veal cutlets, about 5 ounces each

1 teaspoon salt

½ teaspoon pepper

½ to 1 cup flour

2 tablespoons butter or olive oil

2 cups sliced fresh mushrooms

⅔ cup heavy cream

Few drops lemon juice

# Lapin Sauté Chasseur

*Rabbit Sauté Chasseur*

Cut rabbit into twelve pieces as follows: two front legs, the saddle (or back) into four pieces, two back legs each cut into two pieces, and the ribs into two pieces. Season with salt and pepper. ♦ In a large, heavy saucepan or skillet, brown bacon until crisp. Remove from pan, drain, crumble, and set aside. ♦ Sauté rabbit pieces over medium heat in bacon fat left in the pan, browning well on each side. ♦ Add shallots and garlic, cooking for about 1 minute, then sprinkle with flour. Stir well and add thyme and basil. ♦ Deglaze with wine, reduce for 1 minute, add water and tomato sauce, and cook, covered, for 40 minutes over low heat. ♦ Add mushrooms, cover again, and cook for 15 more minutes until rabbit is tender. Garnish with chopped parsley.

*Serves 4.*

1 3-pound rabbit, cut up

1½ teaspoons salt

1 teaspoon pepper

5 slices bacon

5 shallots, chopped

4 cloves garlic, chopped

2 tablespoons flour

1 teaspoon dried thyme

1 teaspoon chopped fresh basil or ½ teaspoon dried basil

1½ cups dry white wine

1½ cups water

1 8-ounce can tomato sauce

1 cup sliced mushrooms

1 tablespoon chopped fresh parsley, for garnish

# GIGOT D'AGNEAU

*Leg of Lamb*

Preheat oven to 450°F. ♦ Season lamb with salt and pepper. With a paring knife, make two incisions into the fleshiest part of the leg and push in two cloves of garlic. Brush lamb with oil and season with rosemary. Set lamb in a roasting pan and sear in oven for 20 minutes or until the whole leg is golden brown. Reduce temperature to 350°F and cook until done. Total cooking time should be 12 minutes per pound for medium rare, (130°F) or 15 minutes per pound for well done (160°F). ♦ Remove lamb from roasting pan and set it on a hot platter. Remove fat from the pan and pour in stock or bouillon. Bring to a boil and scrape up coagulated juices; strain into a hot sauceboat. Garnish with parsley or watercress.

*If you wish, you may substitute Sauce Béarnaise for the pan juices.*

*Serves 8.*

**1 6-pound leg of lamb**

**1 tablespoon salt**

**1 tablespoon pepper**

**2 whole cloves garlic**

**Vegetable oil**

**1 pinch whole rosemary**

**1 cup brown stock or canned beef bouillon**

**Parsley or watercress, for garnish**

**Sauce Béarnaise (optional, see page 104)**

# Selle d'Agneau Louis Viboud

*Saddle of Lamb Louis Viboud*

Preheat oven to 400°F. ♦ Cook spinach in water with 1 teaspoon salt for 2 minutes. Drain and cool; press well to remove excess water. Chop spinach and set aside. ♦ Put 2 tablespoons olive oil in a skillet and set over medium heat. Sauté sausage and liver, seasoning with 1 teaspoon salt and ½ teaspoon pepper. Add shallots and garlic, continue to sauté for 2 minutes, then add chopped spinach and toss well. Add egg. ♦ Place the open lamb saddle on the table and spread with meat and spinach mixture. Roll and tie the saddle. Place the remaining 3 tablespoons olive oil in a roasting pan, set on range over medium high heat, and brown meat on all sides. Season with salt and pepper and place in oven. After 30 minutes, surround lamb with potatoes, onions, and garlic. Roast approximately 1 hour longer, depending on size. Finished dish should be served medium rare, with a center temperature of 160°F. Serve in an earthenware or glass serving dish, with the potatoes and onions all around.

*Serves 6.*

½ pound fresh spinach leaves, stems removed, washed

3 teaspoons salt, divided

5 tablespoons olive oil, divided

1 pound pork sausage

1 pound pork liver

1 teaspoon black pepper, divided

3 shallots, chopped

3 cloves garlic, minced

1 egg, beaten

2½ pounds saddle of lamb, boned, or 5 pounds with bone intact (ask your butcher to trim it)

2 pounds potatoes, peeled and sliced

1 pound onions, peeled and sliced

4 cloves garlic, minced

# Navarin de Mouton Lauragaise

*Mutton Stew*

Season lamb with salt and pepper. In a heavy skillet or thick-bottomed sauce-pan, heat olive oil and sear lamb cubes on all sides. Add oregano and basil. ◆ Add onion and carrots, and continue cooking until onion is translucent. Add garlic. ◆ Sprinkle flour evenly over lamb and mix well. Deglaze with Chablis and bring to a boil. Add tomato sauce and water; mix well. Cover and simmer over low heat for 30 minutes. ◆ Remove lamb to a serving dish. Spoon sauce over lamb and arrange the vegetable garnishes over the top. ◆ This dish is traditionally served with Aubergines à la Provençale (page 87).

*Serves 6.*

**3 pounds boneless lamb shoulder, cut into 2-inch cubes**

**2 teaspoons salt**

**1 teaspoon pepper**

**⅓ cup olive oil**

**1 teaspoon dried oregano**

**1 teaspoon fresh basil or ½ teaspoon dried basil**

**1 large onion, diced**

**2 carrots, julienned**

**3 cloves garlic, minced**

**3 tablespoons flour**

**2 cups Chablis**

**1 8-ounce can tomato sauce**

**2 cups water**

**18 baby carrots, cooked in chicken bouillon, for garnish**

**18 turnips, cut in ball shape and cooked with carrots, for garnish**

**18 potato balls (melon scoop size), cooked in butter, for garnish**

# TOURNEDOS ISMAN BAYELDI

*Fillets Isman Bayeldi*

Season fillets with salt and pepper. ♦ Dredge eggplant slices in flour; roll in beaten egg and bread crumbs. Fry in oil over medium heat and place on two warmed plates. ♦ Add butter to pan and sauté steaks, cooking 4 minutes on each side for medium. Place the steaks on the eggplant slices and, using a spoon or pastry bag, put a dollop of Sauce Béarnaise on top of each fillet. ♦ Accompany with Tomatoes Provençale (page 92).

*This recipe was created by Chef Auguste Escoffier at the Carlton Hotel in London and was named after an Egyptian prince who was a guest there. Jean Paul learned of it from Chef M. Louis Bonfillon, who later served the dish at the Hotel Majestic in Cannes, France.*

*Serves 2.*

**4 3½-ounce beef fillet steaks**

**1 teaspoon salt**

**½ teaspoon pepper**

**4 eggplant slices, ½-inch thick**

**2 small eggs, beaten**

**⅓ cup dry bread crumbs**

**Sauce Béarnaise (see page 104)**

**2 tablespoons vegetable oil**

**2 tablespoons butter**

# Boeuf Bourguignon

*Beef Burgundy*

*I*n a heavy skillet or cast-iron pan, heat oil over medium heat. Add bacon and onions, and cook until they begin to brown. Remove from pan, leaving oil, and set aside. ♦ Increase heat to high. Add beef to pan. Season with salt and pepper, and sauté on all sides until brown. ♦ Add carrots and celery, and continue to cook, covered, for 10 minutes. Sprinkle with flour and mix well. Add garlic, thyme, bay leaf, Burgundy, tomato paste, and the bacon/onion mixture. If wine does not cover the meat, add a little water. Cover and cook slowly over low heat for 2 hours. ♦ Sauté mushrooms in butter over medium-high heat for 3 minutes. Season with salt and pepper to taste ♦ Pour beef into a large bowl or tureen, place mushrooms on top, sprinkle with parsley, and serve over noodles or boiled potatoes.

*This recipe is from the Sahara Hotel and Casino in Lake Tahoe, where one evening Mr. Bienz, food manager for the resort's five restaurants, sampled and was delighted with Jean Paul's Beef Burgundy. The same dish tried later at the hotel's coffee shop, however, was not as satisfying. Mr. Bienz mentioned to the shop's cook that he should learn from Jean Paul, but the cook rightly protested that he must prepare for 500 people. Jean Paul then played a joke on Mr. Bienz, writing an order for Beef Burgundy to serve 4,000 customers that included 2,000 pounds of cubed beef and 100 gallons of Burgundy wine!*

*Serves 6.*

**2 tablespoons oil**

**1 6-ounce slab bacon, diced into ½-inch pieces**

**24 small pearl onions, peeled**

**3 pounds chuck roast, cut into 1-inch cubes**

**1½ teaspoons salt**

**½ teaspoon pepper**

**6 carrots, diced**

**2 ribs celery, diced**

**2 tablespoons flour**

**4 cloves garlic, minced**

**½ teaspoon thyme**

**1 bay leaf**

**3 cups red Burgundy**

**1 tablespoon tomato paste**

**½ pound mushrooms, sliced**

**3 tablespoons butter**

**Parsley, for garnish**

# Pot-au-Feu

*Consommé with Boiled Beef and Vegetables*

Place meat in a large soup kettle and add water to completely cover the meat. Bring to a boil and skim off scum as it surfaces. Stir in salt. ♦ Add remaining ingredients, partially cover the kettle, and simmer for 3 hours. ♦ Strain bouillon through a sieve lined with cheesecloth. ♦ Serve the meat on a large platter with carrots and boiled potatoes or other vegetables all around. Serve the consommé separately in bowls.

*Serves 6.*

**4 pounds beef short ribs or oxtail**

**4 quarts water**

**2 tablespoons salt**

**1 large onion, studded with 3 cloves**

**2 large carrots, cut in half lengthwise**

**2 leeks, leave green tops on**

**2 ribs celery, sliced**

**2 garlic cloves, unpeeled**

**Parsley**

**Pinch of thyme**

**1 bay leaf**

# Boeuf à la Stroganoff

*Beef Stroganoff*

Cut the meat with the grain into strips about 2 inches long and 1 inch thick. Season with salt and pepper. ♦ In a skillet melt butter and oil over medium-high heat. Add meat, and brown well on all sides. Add onions and mushrooms; sauté until onions are translucent and mushrooms are tender. ♦ Sprinkle meat mixture with flour and mix well. Add sherry and simmer for a few minutes to allow alcohol to boil off. Mix in mustard and heavy cream until combined. ♦ Remove meat and mushrooms from the sauce with a slotted spoon. Bring sauce to a simmer and allow to thicken. Arrange meat on a serving platter or a bed of noodles, pour sauce over, and garnish with a dollop of sour cream.

*Serves 6.*

2 pounds beef tenderloin fillet

2 teaspoons salt

1 teaspoon pepper

4 tablespoons butter

2 tablespoons vegetable oil

⅔ cup sliced onion

1½ cups sliced mushrooms

1 tablespoon flour

½ cup sherry

2 teaspoons prepared mustard

⅓ cup heavy cream

⅓ cup sour cream

# LANGUE DE BOEUF GRIBICHE

*Beef Tongue Gribiche*

Trim the fleshy rear underside of the tongue. Place tongue in boiling salted water for 3 minutes, using just enough water to cover the tongue completely. Remove, allow to cool, and peel off skin. ♦ Put skinned tongue back into water and bring back to a boil. Skim surface of water, then add onion, cloves, celery, and carrot. Simmer tongue, covered, for 1 hour or until tender. ♦ Remove tongue when tender and allow to cool completely. Slice into ¼ inch slices and arrange in a long dish with the slices overlapping one another. Spoon Sauce Gribiche over top and serve.

*Serves 6.*

**SAUCE GRIBICHE (GRIBICHE SAUCE):** is 2 cups of Jean Paul Vinaigrette Dressing (page 117) with the addition of 2 chopped hard-boiled eggs and 2 tablespoons of capers. Thicken the dressing with 2 tablespoons of mayonnaise. This is good with cold beef, pork, veal, or turkey.

*1 beef tongue, approximately 2 ½ pounds*

*1 onion, studded with 2 cloves*

*1 rib celery, chopped*

*2 carrots, chopped*

*1 tablespoon salt*

**Sauce Gribiche (see below)**

# Kasteel Franssen Dutch Biefstuk

*Kasteel Franssen Dutch Beefsteak*

Cut the tenderloin into fillet steaks, 3 ounces each (2 steaks per guest). Season with salt and pepper. ♦ In a large sauté pan, melt butter and vegetable oil over medium-high heat. Cook fillets on both sides until evenly browned. ♦ Pour off excess fat; pour brandy over fillets and flame off alcohol. Transfer steaks to serving dish and keep warm. ♦ Return sauté pan to medium-high heat, add shallots, and sauté for 1 minute. Reduce heat and add mustard and heavy cream, stirring until smooth. Bring to a simmer and reduce until cream is slightly thickened. Pour sauce over fillets and serve. ♦ The usual accompaniment to this recipe is buttered noodles or rice pilaf.

*This recipe was created especially for Joe and Elisa Franssen, the Dutch-born owners of the Kasteel Franssen restaurant in Oak Harbor, Washington, which Jean Paul helped to design.*

*Serves 6.*

**2¼ pounds lean beef tenderloin**

**2 teaspoons salt**

**1 teaspoon pepper**

**2 tablespoons butter**

**1 tablespoon vegetable oil**

**⅓ cup brandy**

**3 tablespoons chopped shallots**

**2 tablespoons prepared mustard**

**½ cup heavy cream**

# Pannequets au Jambon

*Crêpes with Ham*

**F**ollow Crêpe recipe to make 12 pannequets. ♦ Melt butter in a sauté pan and cook chopped mushrooms for 3 minutes. Mix in 3 tablespoons of Sauce Béchamel and season with salt and pepper. Remove mixture from the heat and cool. ♦ Preheat oven to 375°F. ♦ Place a thin slice of ham on each crêpe. Spread a thin layer of the mushroom and cream mixture on the sliced ham. Roll up crêpes and arrange together in a buttered ovenproof dish, or place each crêpe in an individual baking dish. Cover crêpes with the remaining Sauce Béchamel and sprinkle with the grated Swiss cheese. Bake until cheese is melted and slightly browned.

*While staying at the Sahara, The Carpenters would often have their parents join them. One of the family's favorite meals was this crêpe dish.*

*Serves 6.*

**12 crêpes (see page 81)**

**FILLING:**

**2 tablespoons butter**

**2 cups finely chopped mushrooms**

**2 cups Sauce Béchamel (see page 107)**

**½ teaspoon salt**

**1 teaspoon pepper**

**12 thin slices cooked ham**

**2 cups grated Swiss cheese**

# POULTRY

*Hotel-Château De La Caze (1949):*
*letter of recommendation given to Jean Paul*
*shortly before he came to America.*

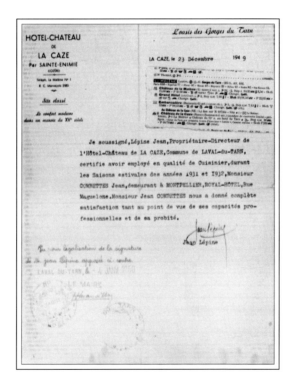

# Canard aux Lentilles

*Duck with Lentils*

Never purchase a duck that is over 5 pounds. Larger ducks tend to be tough, so it is better to purchase two small ducks. ♦ Preheat oven to 450°F. ♦ Season duck, including the cavity, with pepper and 1 tablespoon of the salt, and place breast side up in a roasting pan. Roast uncovered for about 30 minutes or until brown and crisp on the outside. Reduce oven temperature to 375°F and roast for at least 1 hour longer, basting duck in its own juices several times. ♦ While duck is roasting, place lentils in a saucepan, cover with cold water, and add remaining 1 tablespoon salt. Bring to a boil and cook 15 minutes. Drain and set aside. ♦ In a heavy-bottomed pot place 3 tablespoons of liquid fat from the roasting duck. Place pot on top of the stove over low heat; add onion, celery, and carrots, and sauté until soft. Add garlic, sprinkle with flour, and mix well. Stir in tomato sauce. ♦ Add lentils to pot and add just enough water to cover them. Cover and cook over very low heat until lentils are tender, approximately 1 hour. ♦ Remove duck from oven and cut into eight pieces. Place lentils in a serving dish, arrange duck pieces on top, and serve.

*Serves 4.*

1 4- to 5-pound duck, ready to cook

1 teaspoon pepper

2 tablespoons salt, divided

2 cups lentils

1 medium onion, chopped

1 rib celery, chopped

2 medium carrots, chopped

2 cloves garlic, minced

2 tablespoons flour

Salt and pepper, to taste

1 8-ounce can tomato sauce

# Suprêmes de Volaille Champagne aux Morilles

*Chicken Breasts in Champagne Morel Sauce*

Preheat oven to 350°F. ♦ Place chicken breasts between two sheets of waxed paper and pound with the bottom of a skillet to flatten slightly. Season with salt and pepper and dredge in flour, shaking off any excess. ♦ In an ovenproof skillet, heat butter and oil over medium heat and lightly brown both sides of breasts. Set skillet in the oven for about 10 minutes. ♦ Remove skillet from oven and place it back on the stove over low heat. Add mushrooms, cover, and cook 5 more minutes. Remove cover and pour in Champagne or dry sherry. Reduce for a few seconds and add cream. Remove breasts and arrange on a serving platter. Continue to reduce sauce until thick enough to coat breasts. Stir in lemon juice, pour sauce over breasts, and serve.

*Serves 6.*

**6 boneless breasts of chicken**

**1½ teaspoons salt**

**1 teaspoon white pepper**

**2 tablespoons flour**

**2 tablespoons butter**

**2 tablespoons oil**

**2 cups morel mushrooms, washed, dried, and sliced (cultivated mushrooms or chanterelles may be substituted)**

**1 cup Champagne or dry sherry**

**1 cup heavy cream**

**Juice of half a lemon**

# Poulet Languedocienne

*Chicken Languedoc Style*

Preheat oven to 375°F. ♦ Heat olive oil in a heavy 10-inch skillet over medium-high heat. Season chicken pieces with salt and pepper and sauté, skin side down first, until brown on both sides. ♦ Cover skillet and bake for 15 minutes. ♦ Return skillet to top of stove; add shallots and minced garlic. Sauté over low heat for 2 minutes. Deglaze pan with vermouth or Chablis. ♦ Melt butter in a sauté pan over medium heat. Add artichoke hearts. Season with salt and pepper and cook for 5 minutes. ♦ Add artichokes to chicken in skillet, cover, and place skillet in oven for 10 more minutes. ♦ To serve, place chicken in the center of an oval dish. Arrange artichokes and shallots at each end. Pour juice from skillet over chicken pieces, sprinkle with chopped parsley, and serve.

*Serves 4.*

4 tablespoons olive oil

1 4-pound chicken, cut into 6 pieces

20 whole shallots, peeled

4 cloves garlic, minced

1 cup dry vermouth or Chablis

2 tablespoons butter

12 artichoke hearts

1½ teaspoons salt

1 teaspoon pepper

Chopped parsley, for garnish

# Poulet Sauté à la Niçoise

*Chicken Sauté Niçoise*

Preheat oven to 375°F. ◆ Disjoint the chicken into eight pieces: two breasts, two legs, two thighs, and two wings. Season with salt and pepper. In a large skillet heat olive oil and 3 tablespoons of the butter over medium heat. Brown chicken pieces on each side. ◆ Heat 1 quart of water to boiling in a medium saucepan and blanch onions for 1 minute. Remove skins. Add onions to chicken, cover skillet, and place in oven for 15 minutes. ◆ Remove skillet from oven and add tomatoes, garlic, wine, olives, tarragon, thyme, and the ½ cup water. Simmer, covered, on top of stove for 5 minutes. ◆ Sauté artichoke hearts in the remaining 2 tablespoons butter. ◆ Remove chicken pieces from skillet and arrange on a large serving platter. Place onions and artichoke hearts around the edge to form a border. Pour sauce from skillet over chicken pieces and serve.

*Serves 4.*

1 4-pound frying chicken

1½ teaspoons salt

½ teaspoon pepper

4 tablespoons olive oil

5 tablespoons butter, divided

24 pearl onions

3 medium tomatoes, peeled and quartered

3 cloves garlic, minced

1 cup Chablis

18 pitted black olives

½ teaspoon tarragon

½ cup water

1 tablespoon thyme

8 artichoke hearts

# Coq au Vin Bourguignonne

*Chicken Burgundy Style*

Preheat oven to 400°F. Cut chicken into eight pieces: two breasts, two thighs, two legs, and two wings. Bone the breasts. Season chicken with salt and pepper. ♦ Blanch bacon in boiling water for 2 minutes to remove the smoky flavor. Set aside. ♦ In a large skillet, sauté onions and bacon in butter and vegetable oil until golden brown and remove to a plate. In the same butter, lightly sauté mushrooms and remove to plate with onions and bacon. ♦ In the same skillet with the same butter, brown chicken on all sides and then sprinkle with flour. Add garlic, thyme, bay leaf, and basil; stir well and place in oven for 5 minutes. ♦ Add onion-bacon-mushroom garnish, and pour in Burgundy. Add chopped liver, if desired. Bring to a boil, stir lightly, cover, and bake for 30 minutes. ♦ Remove chicken from oven and pour in brandy. Stir lightly. If sauce is too liquid, bind with 2 tablespoons flour mixed with 2 tablespoons butter.

*Serves 4.*

1 large frying chicken (approximately 4 pounds)

2 teaspoons salt

2 teaspoons pepper

¼ pound sliced bacon, chopped

12 pearl onions, skinned

2 tablespoons butter

2 tablespoons vegetable oil

2 cups mushrooms, quartered

2 tablespoons flour

4 cloves garlic, minced

⅔ teaspoon dried thyme

1 bay leaf

1 teaspoon fresh basil, chopped

2 cups Burgundy

2 tablespoons brandy

Chicken liver, chopped (optional)

# CROQUETTES DE VOLAILLE

*Chicken Croquettes*

**All steps except the final frying of the croquettes should be completed the day before.** ♦ Place whole chicken in a stockpot. Cover with cold water and bring to a boil. Reduce heat and simmer 10 minutes. Skim off scum as it surfaces. ♦ Add leek, carrot, celery, parsley, and onion. Cover pot and continue simmering until the chicken is thoroughly cooked, about 45 minutes. ♦ Remove chicken from stock and allow it to cool completely. Remove the skin and bones and discard. Grind or dice chicken meat very finely. ♦ Reduce chicken stock to about 3 cups. In a 1-quart saucepan, make a roux with the oil, 1 cup of the flour, and ¼ cup of the butter, cooking over low heat. Gradually add stock, mixing well with a wire whisk. ♦ Place mushrooms in a skillet in remaining ¼ cup butter and sauté for about 3 minutes. Add chicken and sauce. Mix well, remove from heat, and stir in egg yolks and truffles, if used. When thoroughly mixed, spread mixture evenly in a shallow pan lined with waxed paper. Set in refrigerator and allow to cool completely. ♦ Place the remaining 1 cup flour, the whole beaten eggs, and the bread crumbs in separate shallow bowls. Remove chicken mixture from refrigerator and, using a serving spoon, scoop out an approximate 2-ounce portion. Roll mixture first in the flour, then in the beaten egg, and finally in the bread crumbs. Form each croquette into the shape of a cork, and put back in the refrigerator overnight. ♦ Fry croquettes in 1 inch of hot vegetable oil at 350°F until they are golden brown and crisp on the outside. Serve with Sauce Demi-Glace (page 111) on the side.

*Serves 6.*

1 3-pound chicken, whole

1 leek, coarsely chopped

1 medium carrot, coarsely chopped

1 rib celery, coarsely chopped

3 sprigs parsley

1 medium onion, studded with 2 cloves

2 tablespoons olive oil

2 cups flour, divided

½ cup butter, divided

1½ cups finely chopped mushrooms

3 egg yolks, beaten

1 2-ounce can truffles (optional)

2 whole eggs, beaten

2 cups bread crumbs

Vegetable oil for frying

# Seafood

*Jean Paul, circa 1935, during
his stay at the Majestic Hotel
in Cannes, France.*

# Saumon à la Norvegienne

*Salmon Norwegian Style*

Combine first nine ingredients in a large stockpot and bring to a boil over high heat. Reduce heat and simmer for 10 minutes. ♦ Wrap salmon in cheesecloth, bending it to give the impression of swimming. (Secure the cheesecloth with string tied around the head and tail.) ♦ Carefully lower fish into court bouillon, keeping the curved shape. Bring back to a simmer and allow to cook for 10 minutes. Remove from heat and allow fish to cool completely in the bouillon. ♦ Carefully remove salmon from the pot and place on a wire rack. Remove cheesecloth and skin from body of fish without damaging the head and tail. Place in refrigerator. ♦ Pour 1 quart of the court bouillon into a large saucepan over low heat. Dissolve gelatine in bouillon, stirring constantly with a wire whisk. Bring to a boil and simmer for 3 minutes. Strain into a shallow pan. Mix 1 tablespoon of the gelatine-bouillon mixture with the mayonnaise and keep separate. Chill both the bouillon and the mayonnaise well. ♦ Place salmon upright on a large serving dish. Melt ½ cup of the gelatine/bouillon in a small saucepan over low heat and glaze salmon quickly, giving it a shiny appearance. Chop remaining gelatine/bouillon to a rough consistency and arrange around the fish. ♦ Pipe mayonnaise mixture down spine of salmon, using a pastry bag fitted with a fluted tip. Arrange shrimp with tails up, securing with toothpicks along the backbone. ♦ Place lemon slices around outer rim of serving dish. Put mussels on top of the artichoke bottoms, and alternate with fluted mushrooms around the dish next to the lemon slices. Spoon a small amount of Sauce Béchamel over mussels. Place parsley sprigs and tomato rose; serve buffet style.

*This poached salmon recipe, usually displayed as a centerpiece in a cold buffet, won Jean Paul a first prize in the International Exhibition of the Culinary Arts in 1954.*

*Serves 8 to 10.*

**3 quarts water**

**3 cups white vinegar**

**1 tablespoon black pepper corns**

**2 tablespoons salt**

**1 medium carrot, chopped**

**1 medium onion, chopped**

**1 rib celery, chopped**

**1 teaspoon dried thyme**

**1 bay leaf**

**1 5-pound salmon, cleaned, with head and tail still attached**

**2 envelopes unflavored gelatine**

**1 cup mayonnaise**

**10 shrimp, boiled and peeled, with tails on**

**1 lemon, halved lengthwise and thinly sliced**

**6 mussels, steamed and removed from shells**

**6 artichoke bottoms**

**5 mushroom caps, fluked**

**Sauce Béchamel (see page 107)**

**Tomato rose**

**Parsley sprigs**

# Langouste à L'Albert

*Lobster Albert*

In a 6-quart or larger kettle, bring to a boil the water, vinegar, celery, carrot, leek, thyme, bay leaf, salt, and peppercorns. ♦ Turn lobster on its back and cut in half lengthwise. Remove the black coral and the brownish green tomalley from the cavity; set aside. Tie lobster halves together and cook for 20 minutes in the court bouillon. Remove lobster and allow to cool. ♦ Combine diced shallots and tomatoes and bring to a simmer in a small sauté pan. Season with salt and pepper. ♦ Make a spread by combining the coral and tomalley from the lobster with softened butter, paprika, and tarragon in a small mixing bowl. ♦ Remove lobster meat from shells and dice. Set shells aside. Place lobster meat and tomato/shallot mixture in a large, heavy-bottomed skillet. Sauté over high heat until very hot; remove from heat and add cognac or brandy. Return to very hot burner and burn off alcohol. Douse the flames with skillet cover to prevent mixture from turning bitter. Spoon lobster mixture back into shells and cover with a thin layer of spread. Finish by glazing under a broiler until golden brown.

*Serves 2.*

**1 large live Maine lobster, about 2 pounds**

**4 quarts water**

**1 quart white wine vinegar**

**2 ribs celery, chopped**

**1 large carrot, chopped**

**1 leek, chopped**

**1 teaspoon thyme**

**1 bay leaf**

**1 tablespoon salt**

**1 teaspoon peppercorns**

**3 shallots, finely diced**

**2 medium tomatoes, peeled, seeded, and chopped**

**1 teaspoon salt**

**½ teaspoon pepper**

**2 ounces butter, softened**

**½ teaspoon paprika**

**½ teaspoon chopped fresh tarragon**

**2 ounces Cognac or brandy**

# Scampi à la Jean Paul

*P*reheat broiler. ♦ Peel and devein shrimp and butterfly. Arrange shrimp in two long individual ovenproof casseroles and season lightly with salt and pepper. ♦ In a small saucepan heat butter and minced garlic, simmer over low heat for a few minutes, and spoon over shrimp. Place casseroles under the broiler for 3 minutes. ♦ Pour wine over shrimp; sprinkle with parsley and lemon juice. Broil for 2 more minutes and serve.

*In his original recipe, Jean Paul preferred the large (4 to 6 ounces each) shrimp found only in the Mediterranean Sea off the coasts of Italy and Corsica, but shrimp from the Gulf of Mexico are a good substitute.*

*Serves 2.*

**12 large shrimp (about 1½ pounds)**

**½ teaspoon salt**

**½ teaspoon pepper**

**4 tablespoons melted butter**

**1 teaspoon minced garlic**

**½ cup Chablis or dry vermouth**

**2 teaspoons chopped fresh parsley**

**2 teaspoons lemon juice**

# Champignons au Crabe

*Mushrooms Stuffed with Crab*

*P*reheat oven to 450°F. ♦ In a large skillet melt butter over medium heat. Place mushroom caps top down in the skillet and brown lightly on both sides. Remove and arrange top down on a baking sheet. ♦ Increase temperature to high, add shallots and crab meat to skillet, and sauté for about 1 minute, stirring constantly. You may need to add more butter or oil. Pour over brandy and flame off immediately. ♦ Pour in heavy cream and reduce heat to a simmer. Allow cream mixture to reduce until almost dry. Season with salt and pepper to taste and remove from heat. ♦ Spoon crab mixture into mushroom caps. Cover the stuffed mushrooms with Sauce Hollandaise. Place baking sheet on upper rack of oven. Bake until golden brown on top. Remove from oven and serve.

*Serves 6 as a entreé, or makes 24 appetizers.*

**24 large mushroom caps**

**2 tablespoons butter**

**4 tablespoons chopped shallots**

**2 cups crab meat, fresh, frozen, or canned**

**2 tablespoons brandy**

**½ cup heavy cream**

**Salt and white pepper to taste**

**1 cup Sauce Hollandaise (see page 109)**

# TRUITE AU BLEU

*Trout in Blue Coat*

To prepare the court bouillon, combine the first eight ingredients, bring to a boil, and cook for 8 to 10 minutes. ♦ The trout must be live and removed from the water no more than 15 minutes before it is to be served. ♦ Kill the trout with a blow to the back of the head; open the belly with a sharp knife and remove the intestines and the gills. Do not wash the trout and do not wipe! You must not remove the viscosity of the skin, which is what creates the blue color. ♦ Drop trout immediately into the boiling court bouillon and simmer for 8 minutes. The trout will shrink immediately; do not worry if the skin breaks. Drain the trout and serve on a cloth napkin surrounded with parsley. Serve with quartered lemon and melted butter on the side.

*If live trout is available, this makes a unique dish for entertaining. When prepared properly, the fish will turn a beautiful blue color, due to the reaction of the vinegar court bouillon with the natural viscosity of fish skin. Fish that is bought fresh at a fish market will have the same flavor but will lack the brilliant blue hue that comes only when fish is killed within 15 minutes of preparation.*

*Serves 2 to 4.*

**2 quarts water**

**1 cup vinegar**

**1 small onion, sliced**

**1 carrot, sliced**

**Pinch of dry thyme or sprig of fresh thyme**

**1 bay leaf**

**1 tablespoon salt**

**1 teaspoon peppercorns**

**2 12-ounce trout, very fresh**

**Parsley, for garnish**

**1 lemon, quartered**

**Melted warm butter**

# Filets de Sole au Noilly

*Fillets of Sole Vermouth*

Preheat oven to 350°F. ♦ Butter the bottom of a baking dish. Season fillets with salt and pepper and arrange in baking dish. Sprinkle shallots and mushrooms on top and pour vermouth over fillets. Butter a piece of waxed paper and place buttered side down on fillets. Bake 10 minutes or until fillets are firm to the touch. Remove from the oven. ♦ Drain stock into a saucepan and boil over medium heat until reduced to 1 cup. ♦ In a small bowl mix ½ cup of softened butter and flour with a fork to make a *beurre manié*. ♦ Add the *beurre manié* to the boiling stock, stirring well with a wire whisk. Gradually stir in cream, and add lemon juice. Sauce should be thick enough to coat fish. ♦ Just before serving, reheat the fillets covered with buttered waxed paper and set in oven to keep warm. Spoon sauce over fillets and serve immediately. ♦ For a nice presentation of this dish, make a cordon of Duchesse Potatoes (page 95) all around the plate and set under the broiler until nicely browned.

*Serves 6.*

**½ cup plus additional softened butter**

**12 fillets Dover or Petrale sole (3-ounce average size)**

**1½ teaspoons salt**

**½ teaspoon white pepper**

**½ cup chopped shallots**

**1½ cups sliced fresh mushrooms**

**1½ cups dry vermouth**

**½ cup flour**

**¼ cup heavy cream**

**1 tablespoon lemon juice**

# FILET DE SOLE CLARENCE

*Fillet of Sole Clarence*

Preheat oven to 375°F. ♦ Separate mushroom caps from stems; chop stems finely and set aside. Cook mushroom caps in boiling water with lemon juice added for 1 minute; set aside. ♦ Place sole fillets in a large, ovenproof skillet that has been lightly coated with butter. Spread shallots and chopped mushroom stems over the top, and season with salt and pepper. Pour Chablis over fillets and cover with a piece of lightly buttered waxed paper, buttered side down. Place skillet in oven for 10 minutes or until fillets are firm to touch when pressed with a finger. ♦ Arrange fillets neatly on a large, ovenproof platter. Place skillet back on the stove over low heat and reduce cooking liquid to about ¼ cup. Meanwhile, with a pastry bag, pipe a border of Duchesse Potatoes around the fillets. ♦ When stock is reduced, gradually whisk in Sauce Mornay and heavy cream until combined. Allow to thicken slightly. ♦ Spoon sauce over fillets and arrange mushroom caps neatly around the dish. Sprinkle Parmesan cheese over the top, and place under the broiler for approximately 2 minutes or until the sauce and potatoes are nicely browned.

*Serves 6.*

**12 mushrooms**

**1 tablespoon lemon juice**

**6 6-ounce fillets of sole**

**2 tablespoons butter**

**½ cup chopped shallots**

**1½ teaspoons salt**

**1 teaspoon white pepper**

**1 cup Chablis**

**Duchesse Potatoes
(see page 95)**

**2 cups Sauce Mornay
(see page 108)**

**½ cup heavy cream**

**½ cup grated Parmesan cheese**

# Brochette de Fruits de Mer La Rotonde

*Seafood on Skewers*

Cook shrimp in simmering water with salt and lemon juice for 1 minute, then cool immediately under cold running water. ♦ Poach mussels and oysters in a large skillet with Chablis and water, covered, over low heat, until shells open. Remove shellfish from shells. ♦ On each of six 5-inch bamboo skewers, alternate two shrimp, two mussels, two oysters, and two scallops; lightly season with salt and pepper. Roll skewers in flour, then in eggs, and finally in bread crumbs until well coated. Spread a small amount of mustard on each skewer. Cook the skewers in a large sauté pan in the butter and oil over medium heat until both sides are golden brown.

*The fashionable and luxurious La Rotonde Restaurant at the Grand Hotel in Sète, France, included many Provençal dishes on its menu. The Brochette is one such traditional recipe.*

*Serves 6.*

**12 large shrimp, peeled and deveined**

**1 teaspoon salt**

**1 tablespoon lemon juice**

**12 mussels**

**12 medium oysters**

**¼ cup Chablis**

**¼ cup water**

**12 sea scallops**

**Salt and pepper to taste**

**1 cup flour**

**3 eggs, beaten**

**1 cup bread crumbs**

**2 tablespoons Dijon mustard**

**2 tablespoons butter**

**2 tablespoons oil**

# Rouget de la Méditerranée Toulonaise

*Mediterranean Red Mullet Toulon Style*

Season fish with 1½ teaspoons salt and ½ teaspoon pepper. Flour lightly and brown quickly over medium high heat on both sides in skillet with olive oil. Remove mullet to a plate. ♦ Reduce heat to medium, add onion to skillet, and sauté slowly until light brown. Add tomatoes, season with 1 teaspoon salt and ½ teaspoon pepper, and add garlic and basil. Cook until tomatoes turn into pulp. ♦ Spread tomato sauce in the bottom of an ovenproof serving dish. Place fish on top of tomato and sprinkle with lemon juice. Bake 3 minutes at 450°F. ♦ Remove dish from oven, sprinkle with parsley, and pour melted butter over the mullet.

*The red mullet is one of the finest fish in the Mediterranean, a rockfish of very delicate flavor. On the French Riviera, mullet is cleaned, without removing the scales, and then sprinkled with olive oil and grilled. This simple method is favored in Provençe as well.*

*Serves 6.*

**6 large (1 to 2 pounds) red mullet (sometimes called goatfish)**

**2½ teaspoons salt, divided**

**1 teaspoon pepper, divided**

**½ cup flour**

**2 tablespoons olive oil**

**1 onion, chopped**

**4 medium tomatoes, peeled, seeded, and chopped**

**3 cloves garlic, minced**

**1 teaspoon chopped fresh basil**

**Juice of 1 lemon**

**1 teaspoon chopped fresh parsley**

**2 tablespoons melted butter**

# FILET DE TURBOT AU VERMOUTH

*Fillet of Turbot*

reheat oven to 400°F. ♦ Arrange fillets in a buttered casserole and season with salt and pepper. Pour vermouth, lemon juice, and the 1 tablespoon of melted butter over top of fillets. Make sure fillets are almost completely covered with liquid. Cover casserole with foil and bake 12 minutes. ♦ Remove casserole from oven and carefully transfer fillets to a serving platter. Keep in a warm place. Pour poaching liquid into a saucepan, add shallots, and reduce over medium heat to ½ cup. ♦ Transfer liquid to a stainless steel bowl. Whisk in egg yolks and cream. Place bowl in a pan containing 2 inches of simmering water and whisk continuously until sauce begins to thicken. When sauce is thick enough to coat fillets, gradually whisk in clarified butter to form an emulsion and then add cayenne. Spoon sauce over fillets. Garnish with Duchesse Potatoes and place under the broiler for approximately 2 minutes or until the sauce and potatoes are nicely browned.

*Serves 6.*

6 6-ounce turbot fillets (English sole or pompano may be substituted)

1 teaspoon salt

½ teaspoon white pepper

2 cups dry vermouth

3 tablespoons lemon juice

1 tablespoon melted butter

3 tablespoons chopped shallots

3 egg yolks

2 tablespoons heavy cream

1 cup clarified butter

Dash cayenne pepper

Duchesse Potatoes (see page 95)

# Salt Codfish Montpellieraine

*P*reheat oven to 375°F. ♦ Place codfish fillets in cold water to soak for 8 hours. Within that time period, change the water completely twice. ♦ Place fillets in a skillet, add water to cover, and bring to a boil. Simmer 2 to 3 minutes, then remove fillets carefully. Drain and set aside. Watch time carefully — if the fillets are left in for too long, they will become tough. ♦ Sauté sliced onion in olive oil (reserving 1 tablespoon of the oil) until lightly browned. Add spinach and garlic; season with salt and pepper. Continue cooking until spinach is limp and barely tender. ♦ Spread spinach and onion mixture on the bottom of a baking dish. Place the fillets on top and cover with Sauce Mornay. Sprinkle bread crumbs over top and moisten with reserved olive oil. Bake for 15 minutes or until bread crumbs turn golden brown.

*Serves 6.*

**2 pounds salt codfish fillets**

**1 large onion, sliced**

**½ cup olive oil**

**2 pounds fresh spinach leaves, julienned**

**4 cloves garlic, minced**

**Salt and pepper to taste**

**1 pint Sauce Mornay (see page 108)**

**½ cup bread crumbs**

# Bourride á la Sétoise

*Whitefish Sète Style*

Place water, Chablis, onion, leek, salt, and peppercorns in a 4-quart saucepan. Bring to a boil, cover, and cook 15 minutes. ♦ Add fish to stock, bring to a boil, and simmer about 5 minutes. ♦ With a slotted spatula, gently remove fish from stock and place on a platter; keep warm. Reduce stock to ½ cup and allow to cool for a few minutes. ♦ In a blender or food processor, mix egg yolks and bread crumbs at medium speed. Add Aïoli, switch to high speed, and gradually add remaining stock. ♦ To serve, alternate fish fillets and croutons on a platter and cover with sauce. Garnish with fresh parsley and serve immediately.

*Serves 6.*

**6 cups water**

**2 cups Chablis**

**1 large onion, chopped**

**1 leek, chopped**

**1 teaspoon salt**

**1 teaspoon peppercorns**

**3 pounds cod or halibut fillet (about 6 8-ounce fillets)**

**3 egg yolks**

**1 tablespoon fine bread crumbs**

**1 cup Aïoli (see page 114)**

**6 croutons (see Onion Soup recipe, page 22)**

**Parsley, for garnish**

# Coquilles Saint-Jacques

*Sea Scallops Saint-Jacques*

In a medium sauté pan, heat 1 tablespoon of the butter over medium heat. Add mushrooms and shallots and sauté for 3 minutes. Remove pan from stove and divide mushrooms among six scallop shells. ♦ Return pan to the stove and add vermouth or Chablis, lemon juice, basil, salt, and pepper. Bring liquid to a simmer. Add scallops and poach for about 1 minute. Remove scallops, using a slotted spoon, and divide them evenly among the six shells. ♦ Reduce cooking liquid to about 1 cup. In a separate bowl, combine the remaining 1 tablespoon of butter and the flour until mixed; stir into the liquid until dissolved. Spoon sauce over scallops. Sprinkle each shell evenly with bread crumbs and Parmesan cheese. Spoon clarified butter evenly over the top of each shell and place under broiler for 1 minute or until top turns golden brown.

*Serves 6.*

**2 tablespoons butter, divided**

**½ pound mushrooms, sliced**

**2 tablespoons chopped shallots**

**1¼ cups dry vermouth or Chablis**

**1 tablespoon lemon juice**

**1 teaspoon fresh basil or ½ teaspoon dried basil**

**1 teaspoon salt**

**½ teaspoon pepper**

**2 pounds sea scallops (about 30 medium-sized)**

**3 tablespoons flour**

**4 tablespoons grated Parmesan cheese**

**4 tablespoons bread crumbs**

**2 tablespoons clarified butter**

# Moules Marinière

*Mussels Marinière*

Scrape, wash, and debeard mussels under cold running water. ♦ Place mussels in a large stockpot and pour in white wine, lemon juice, and water. Sprinkle with the shallots, thyme, basil, parsley, and pepper. Cover and cook over high heat. Bring liquid to a boil and stir mussels several times, ensuring that all mussels are cooked. When the shells open they are cooked. Discard any that do not open. Remove pot from heat and allow mussels to cool slightly. ♦ Remove mussels from pot, reserving broth. Remove the top half of each shell. Place mussels in their half shells in a serving dish and keep warm. ♦ In a sauté pan, melt butter and stir in flour over low heat to form a roux. Strain in the reserved broth gradually, whisking well until sauce is thickened. Simmer for 15 minutes and adjust seasonings. ♦ Pour sauce over mussels, sprinkle with fresh parsley, and serve. ♦ May be served with toasted garlic bread.

*Jean Paul used this recipe when creating menus for the Kasteel Franssen in Oak Harbor, Washington, where it became a house specialty.*

*Serves 6.*

**5 pounds mussels**

**1½ cups dry white wine (Chablis type)**

**¼ cup lemon juice**

**½ cup water**

**4 shallots, finely diced**

**½ teaspoon thyme**

**1 teaspoon fresh basil or ½ teaspoon dried basil**

**2 tablespoons chopped fresh parsley**

**2 teaspoons ground black pepper**

**3 tablespoons butter**

**4 tablespoons flour**

**Chopped fresh parsley, for garnish**

# Spaghetti à la Marinare Avec Clovis

*Spaghetti à la Marinare With Clams*

Heat olive oil in a saucepan over medium heat. Sauté onion until lightly browned. Add garlic and tomato, and simmer 2 minutes. Add clams, anchovy, pepper, and basil. ♦ Cook spaghetti in boiling salted water for 15 minutes; rinse under cold running water and drain. ♦ Pour sauce over spaghetti and add grated Parmesan or Romano cheese. Serve.

*Serves 6.*

½ cup olive oil

2 tablespoons chopped onion

1 tablespoon chopped garlic

1 tomato, peeled, seeded, and diced

24 small steamed butter clams in their shells

1 tablespoon chopped anchovy

½ teaspoon pepper

1 teaspoon fresh sweet basil, chopped

1 pound spaghetti

1½ tablespoons salt

1 cup grated Parmesan or Romano cheese

# Bouillabaisse

In a large skillet heat olive oil over medium heat. Add leeks, onion, celery, and garlic; sauté for approximately 5 minutes or until vegetables are tender. ♦ Add all shellfish and fish. Season with salt, pepper, and herbs and continue to sauté for another 2 minutes. Add saffron, if used. ♦ Add Chablis, tomatoes, clam juice, and enough water to cover seafood. Cover pan and reduce heat to simmer for approximately 10 minutes or until fish is cooked. Add creole seasoning to taste, if used. Adjust seasonings. ♦ Divide fish and shellfish among six soup bowls. Ladle bouillon into bowls and serve with toasted French bread. ♦ This dish may be accompanied by a rice pilaf.

*Much of the cuisine of southern France represents tradition and regional flavor, but Bouillabaisse is truly the symbol of Provençe and Languedoc. The Romans first made the stew with fish found in the Mediterranean, prawns, lobsters, garlic, herbs, tomatoes, and olive oil. The same preparation and ingredients are still used today. Any variety of small saltwater fish or rockfish can be used: hogfish, angler, whiting, red snapper, rock cod, sea bass, or halibut. Shellfish such as lobster, prawns, mussels, or sea scallops should also be included. Jean Paul's recipe won first place in 1987 in the "open seafood" category of the West Coast Chowder Challenge in Bellingham, Washington.*

*Serves 6.*

**5 tablespoons olive oil**

**2 leeks, diced**

**1 onion, diced**

**2 ribs celery, diced**

**5 cloves garlic, minced**

**12 large prawns**

**18 sea scallops**

**24 mussels**

**2 pounds halibut, rock cod, sea bass, or snapper, in 6 equal-sized pieces**

**2 pounds striped bass in 6 equal-sized pieces**

**2 teaspoons salt**

**1 teaspoon pepper**

**½ to 1 tablespoon each fresh thyme and fresh basil**

**½ teaspoon saffron (optional)**

**1 cup Chablis**

**2 large tomatoes, peeled, seeded, and chopped**

**1 12-ounce can clam juice**

**Water**

**Sprinkle of creole seasoning (optional)**

**12 slices toasted French bread**

# EGG DISHES

*Jean Paul in 1947,*
*Sète France.*

# Soufflé au Fromage

*Cheese Soufflé*

Melt butter in a 2-quart nonreactive saucepan over low heat. Whisk in flour to form a roux. ♦ Heat milk until scalding and gradually pour it into the roux, whisking constantly to remove any lumps. Add salt and pepper and simmer over low heat for 15 minutes until very thick. ♦ Preheat oven to 400°F. ♦ In a separate bowl, whisk egg yolks. Remove cream mixture from the heat and beat a few spoonfulls into egg yolks; then gradually whisk yolk into sauce. Stir in Swiss cheese until thoroughly mixed. ♦ Beat egg whites until they form semi-stiff peaks; add cream of tartar. Fold whipped egg whites gently into cream sauce and add a dash of nutmeg. ♦ Butter six individual soufflé molds and sprinkle with Parmesan cheese. Spoon soufflé mixture into molds until three-fourths full. Set molds on center rack of oven and reduce temperature immediately to 375°F. ♦ Do not open oven door for at least 20 minutes. Bake until soufflés rise above the molds and turn golden brown on top. Test doneness by inserting a skewer into the side of a soufflé; it should come out relatively clean. Remove from oven and serve immediately.

*Serves 6.*

**3 tablespoons butter**

**3 tablespoons flour**

**1½ cups milk**

**1½ teaspoons salt**

**½ teaspoon white pepper**

**4 eggs, separated**

**¾ cup grated Swiss cheese**

**½ teaspoon cream of tartar**

**Dash of nutmeg**

**⅓ cup grated Parmesan cheese**

**1 tablespoon butter**

# CRÊPES

Combine flour and salt in a medium-sized mixing bowl. ♦ Whisk eggs in a separate bowl. Gradually add milk and continue whisking until combined. Pour egg mixture into flour mixture, whisking until smooth. ♦ Whisk in melted butter until combined. Set batter in refrigerator for 30 minutes before use. ♦ Brush a 6-inch frying pan with clarified butter and place over high heat. Pour in about 2 tablespoons of crêpe batter, swirling pan to coat bottom with a thin film. ♦ Cook the crêpe for about 1 minute, until set and lightly browned on the bottom. Carefully, with a spatula, turn the crêpe and cook for about 30 seconds more, until underside is lightly browned. Turn the crêpe out onto a paper towel. Continue until all crêpes are cooked. ♦ The crêpe is used in many recipes, including Pannequets au Jambon (page 54).

*Makes 12 crêpes.*

**1½ cups all-purpose flour, sifted**

**1 teaspoon salt**

**4 whole eggs**

**1½ cups milk**

**2 tablespoons melted butter**

**1 tablespoon clarified butter**

# Quiche Lorraine

Sift flour into a large mixing bowl and add butter and shortening; mix together with fingers until a lumpy, corn meal–type consistency is reached. Dissolve salt in cold water; add to dough and continue mixing with your hands until a soft dough is formed. ◆ Roll dough out onto a floured cutting board, and knead with the heels of your hands until dough can be shaped into a smooth ball. Cover with plastic wrap and refrigerate for at least 30 minutes. Roll dough out on a lightly floured cutting board to ¼-inch thickness and carefully place in a 10-inch pie pan. ◆ Preheat oven to 400°F. ◆ Cook bacon and diced ham in a sauté pan over medium heat until bacon is crisp; drain on paper towels. Sprinkle bacon and ham evenly into pastry shell. ◆ In a separate, medium-sized mixing bowl, whisk together eggs, nutmeg, salt, and pepper. Gradually whisk in half-and-half until fully incorporated. Pour mixture into pastry-lined pie pan. Sprinkle evenly with grated cheese, and bake 45 minutes or until top is browned and center is cooked. (A knife or toothpick inserted into the center should come out clean.) Serve.

*This dish originated in Lorraine, an eastern province of France near the Rhine River. In medieval times quiche was called simply a "cheese tart."*

*Serves 6 to 8.*

**PASTRY:**

*2 cups all-purpose flour*

*1 4-ounce stick butter, softened*

*2 tablespoons chilled shortening*

*⅓ cup cold water*

*1 teaspoon salt*

**FILLING:**

*8 slices bacon, chopped*

*4 ounces ham, diced*

*4 whole eggs*

*⅓ teaspoon nutmeg*

*1 teaspoon salt*

*⅓ teaspoon pepper*

*2 cups half-and-half*

*1½ cups grated Gruyère cheese*

# Quiche à l'Oignon

*Onion Quiche*

Cook bacon in a sauté pan until crisp. Drain on paper towels, and crumble into pastry shell. ♦ Preheat oven to 350°F. ♦ Sauté onions in olive oil until translucent and tender. Sprinkle flour, salt, pepper, and nutmeg over onions and stir together. Lightly beat cream and eggs together and pour over onions. Bring mixture to a simmer over a low heat, and continue stirring until mixture begins to coagulate. ♦ Pour into quiche pastry shell and sprinkle grated Swiss cheese evenly on top. Bake on bottom rack of oven for 25 to 35 minutes or until a silver knife blade inserted just to the side of center comes out clean.

*Serves 8.*

**1 pastry shell (Quiche Lorraine, see recipe page 82)**

**6 slices bacon**

**4 medium onions, thinly sliced**

**2 tablespoons olive oil**

**1 tablespoon flour**

**1 teaspoon salt**

**¼ teaspoon white pepper**

**⅓ teaspoon nutmeg**

**1 cup heavy cream**

**2 eggs**

**1¾ cups grated Swiss cheese**

# Oeufs à la Chimay

*Eggs à la Chimay*

Hard-boil eggs and remove shells. Cut eggs in half lengthwise and carefully remove yolks. Chop egg yolks very finely. ♦ Sauté mushrooms in 2 tablespoons of the butter over medium heat for 2 minutes or until tender. Add egg yolks and 3 tablespoons of the Sauce Mornay, mixing well. ♦ Preheat oven to 400°F. ♦ Stuff egg whites with mushroom mixture and arrange in a 9- by 12-inch baking dish. Spoon remaining Sauce Mornay over each egg, sprinkle with Swiss cheese, dot tops with remaining butter, and bake until golden brown.

*Serves 6.*

*6 eggs*

*½ pound fresh mushrooms, finely chopped*

*6 tablespoons butter, divided*

*2 cups Sauce Mornay (see page 108), divided*

*1 cup grated Swiss cheese*

# Croque-Monsieur

*Gentleman's Bite*

Grill bread and spread with butter. Cover one slice with Gruyère, then ham, and then blue cheese. Cover sandwich with second slice of bread. ♦ Dip sandwich in egg; fry in butter and oil over medium heat. Cut in half and serve.

*1 Sandwich.*

**2 slices bread**

**1 teaspoon butter**

**1 thin slice Gruyère cheese**

**1 slice boiled ham**

**1 thin slice blue cheese**

**1 egg, beaten**

**1 tablespoon butter**

**1 tablespoon vegetable oil**

# Vegetables

*The Grand Hotel in Sète, France (1950)
where Jean Paul was Executive
Chef for 5 years.*

# Aubergines à la Provençale

*Eggplant Provençale*

Peel eggplants and cut into slices ⅓-inch thick. Sprinkle with salt and place in a colander to drain for 30 minutes. ♦ Remove eggplant slices from colander and wipe off with paper towels. Dredge in flour and sauté each side in ¼ cup of the olive oil. Remove to a serving platter and keep warm. ♦ Heat the remaining ¼ cup olive oil in a saucepan and sauté the tomatoes. Add garlic, salt, and pepper; cook over medium heat for 3 minutes. ♦ Place eggplant slices on a serving dish, spoon tomato sauce evenly over top, and serve.

*Serves 6.*

*2 medium eggplants*

*1 tablespoon salt*

*⅓ cup flour*

*½ cup olive oil, divided*

*3 medium tomatoes, peeled, seeded and chopped*

*3 cloves garlic, minced*

*Salt to taste*

*½ teaspoon pepper*

*3 sprigs parsley, chopped*

# RATATOUILLE NIÇOISE

*Ratatouille*

Peel and dice eggplant into ¼-inch cubes. Place in bowl and toss with salt. Let stand 30 minutes and drain off juice. ♦ Peel and dice zucchini into ¼-inch cubes. Sauté zucchini and eggplant in 1½ tablespoons of the olive oil, browning slightly. ♦ In a separate skillet, cook onions and green pepper in the remaining 1½ tablespoons of olive oil until tender. Add garlic and basil, and season with salt and pepper. ♦ Preheat oven to 350°F. ♦ Add tomatoes to onion and green pepper, and cook, covered, 5 minutes over low heat. ♦ Place one-third of tomato mixture in a 2-quart fireproof casserole. Sprinkle with parsley and layer with half the eggplant/zucchini mixture. On top of that place half the remaining tomato mixture, sprinkle with parsley, then add the remaining eggplant/zucchini mixture, and finish with the last of the tomato mixture and parsley. ♦ Cover casserole and bake 10 minutes. Adjust seasoning and cook uncovered for 10 more minutes.

*One of the great dishes of the Mediterranean, this recipe will fill the kitchen with the herbal aroma of the Provençal coast.*

*Serves 4.*

1 large eggplant

2 tablespoons salt

1 large zucchini

3 tablespoons olive oil, divided

1½ cups diced onions

1½ cups diced green pepper

3 cloves garlic, minced

3 sprigs fresh basil, chopped

2 teaspoons salt

1 teaspoon pepper

1 pound tomatoes, peeled, seeded, and diced

¾ cup chopped fresh parsley

# Artichauts Provençale

*Artichokes Provençale*

Remove outside leaves and stems from bottoms of artichokes. In a thick-bottomed skillet, turn artichokes in olive oil over low heat for a few minutes. Season with salt and pepper, cover, and cook about 10 minutes. ♦ Add lettuce, peas, and water. Cover and continue to simmer over low heat 15 minutes or until artichokes are tender.

*Elvis Presley performed at the Sahara in 1972, and Jean Paul was dutifully informed that "the King" never ate vegetables. At one meal, however, he took the liberty of including this dish on Elvis's room-service cart. The following day, a bodyguard appeared with a $20 bill and a request that Elvis be served the same dish every night for the rest of his stay.*

*Serves 6.*

**24 baby artichokes**

**4 tablespoons olive oil**

**1 tablespoon salt**

**½ teaspoon pepper**

**1 large head Boston or butter lettuce, shredded**

**2 cups peas, shelled**

**½ cup water**

# Artichauts à la Marinade

*Marinated Artichokes*

Cut off the top third of each artichoke and discard. Remove lower, outer leaves and cut artichokes in half lengthwise. Remove the choke (center) of each. If baby artichokes can be found, trim and cook without cutting off tops or removing chokes. ♦ Immediately blanch for 3 minutes in boiling salted water and drain well. (If the cut artichoke is exposed to air before blanching, it will quickly become discolored.) ♦ In a large stainless steel or enamel pot, prepare a court bouillon with 2 cups water, olive oil, Chablis, lemon juice, white peppercorns, coriander seeds, and fennel. Cook the artichokes, covered, in this court bouillon for 25 minutes. Transfer artichokes to an earthenware dish and cover with the strained court bouillon. Chill well and serve.

*Garnishes 4 to 6 entrées.*

**6 medium artichokes or 24 baby artichokes**

**2 cups water**

**½ cup olive oil**

**1 cup Chablis**

**Juice of 2 lemons**

**1 teaspoon white peppercorns**

**1 teaspoon coriander seeds**

**1 stalk fennel**

**1 tablespoon salt**

# CÈPES À LA PROVENÇALE

*Wild Mushrooms Provençale*

Wash and dry mushrooms. Cut in half lengthwise, leaving caps attached to stems. ♦ In a sauté pan, heat olive oil over medium-high heat and add mushrooms. Season with salt and pepper, and cook, stirring occasionally, until mushrooms turn golden brown. ♦ Reduce heat to low and add garlic, bread crumbs, and parsley (reserving some for the garnish). Continue cooking for 2 minutes, stirring occasionally. Sprinkle with remaining parsley and lemon juice. Place in a bowl and serve.

*Cèpes (known in Italy as* porcini *and in Germany as* Steinpilz*) are known to wild mushroom gatherers, including those in the Pacific Northwest, by their scientific name,* Boletus edulis. *They are one of the most savory of all wild mushrooms. Cèpes à la Provençale are traditionally served as an accompaniment for beef or chicken entrées.*

*Serves 6.*

**1 pound cèpes, or other similar wild mushrooms**

**4 tablespoons olive oil**

**1½ teaspoons salt**

**½ teaspoon pepper**

**2 teaspoons minced garlic**

**2 tablespoons bread crumbs**

**1 tablespoon chopped fresh parsley**

**1 tablespoon lemon juice**

# Tomates Provençale

*Tomatoes Provençale*

Slice tomatoes in half horizontally, squeeze out seeds, and sprinkle with garlic, parsley, and bread crumbs. Broil for about 2 minutes until golden brown. Serve.

*Serves 2.*

**2 medium tomatoes**

**2 cloves garlic, minced**

**1 tablespoon chopped fresh parsley**

**⅓ cup bread crumbs**

# TOMATES ANTIBOISE

*Tomatoes Antiboise*

Boil eggs in water until hard. Remove shells and set aside. ♦ Core tomatoes and make a small cross cut on the bottom of each. In a pan, boil enough water to cover the tomatoes. Immerse tomatoes in boiling water for 20 to 30 seconds; then remove and submerge in ice water. ♦ Remove tomatoes from ice water after 1 minute and peel. Cut each tomato in half horizontally and gently squeeze out seeds. ♦ Chop tuna and eggs. Place together in a mixing bowl, add mayonnaise, salt, pepper, parsley, and dill, and mix well with a spoon. Stuff the individual tomato halves with the filling. ♦ Place two tomato halves on lettuce leaves on each plate and garnish with a lemon wedge.

**TOMATES À L'ECOSSAISE (TOMATOES À L'ECOSSAISE):** Follow the same procedure as for Tomates Antiboise, but replace the tuna with cooked salmon. Also add a few drops of Worcestershire sauce to the filling.

*Serves 6.*

2 eggs

6 medium tomatoes

7 ounces white tuna packed in oil, drained

4 tablespoons mayonnaise

Salt to taste

½ teaspoon pepper

2 tablespoons chopped fresh parsley

1 teaspoon chopped fresh dill

Lettuce leaves and lemon wedges, for garnish

# Gratin Dauphinois

*Au Gratin Potatoes*

Preheat oven to 375°F. ♦ Peel and thinly slice potatoes. Arrange slices in a buttered casserole. In a separate bowl whisk together egg yolks, half-and-half, salt, pepper, and ½ cup of the Swiss cheese. Pour over potatoes and top with remaining Swiss cheese. Dot with butter and bake until cheese is bubbly and golden brown, about 1 hour. ♦ Remove from oven and cover with aluminum foil. Return to oven for 30 minutes or until potatoes are easily pierced with a knife.

*Serves 6.*

6 medium-sized potatoes

2 egg yolks, beaten

1½ cups half-and-half

1 teaspoon salt

½ teaspoon white pepper

1½ cups grated Swiss cheese

2 tablespoons butter

# POMMES DE TERRE DUCHESSE

*Duchesse Potatoes*

eel and cut up potatoes; cook in salted water until tender, about 20 minutes. ♦ Drain potatoes and put in food processor or electric mixer. Add butter, pepper, and egg yolks, and work well with a wooden spoon until potatoes have the consistency of a paste. ♦ Place under the broiler until lightly browned. Serve.

*Garnishes 4 to 6 entrées.*

**2 pounds potatoes**

**1 teaspoon salt**

**2 tablespoons butter**

**½ teaspoon white pepper**

**3 egg yolks**

# Pommes de Terre Boulangère

*Potatoes Boulangère*

*P*reheat oven to 350°F. ♦ Peel and thinly slice potatoes. Arrange slices in a buttered casserole and season with salt and pepper. Fill casserole with beef bouillon to three-fourths of the depth of the potatoes. Spread onion slices over top and dot with butter. Bake 30 minutes and serve.

*Serves 6.*

**6 medium-sized potatoes**

**1 teaspoon salt**

**1½ teaspoons pepper**

**1 12-ounce can beef bouillon**

**1 medium onion, thinly sliced**

**2 tablespoons butter**

# Accompaniments

*The Hotel Gallia (1950) in Lourdes, France where Jean Paul was Chef during the summer before coming to America.*

# Gnocchi à la Parisienne

*Dumplings Parisienne Style*

In a saucepan bring to a boil milk, butter, flour, salt, and nutmeg. Mix well with a wooden spatula, until the mixture starts to detach from the sides of the saucepan. Remove from heat and add eggs one at a time, stirring well after each. ♦ Preheat oven to 375°F. ♦ Bring 2 quarts of salted water to a boil. Drop rounded teaspoons of the dough into the simmering water. Cook for 5 minutes or until gnocchi rise to the surface. Using a slotted spoon, remove from water to a dry towel. ♦ Place gnocchi in a well-buttered, shallow baking dish. Spoon Sauce Béchamel over them, sprinkle with Parmesan or Romano cheese, and add a few dots of butter over the top. Bake uncovered until golden brown. Serve immediately.

*Serves 6.*

1 cup milk

½ cup butter

1 cup flour

2 teaspoons salt

½ teaspoon nutmeg

4 eggs

1½ cups Sauce Béchamel (see page 107)

½ cup Parmesan or Romano cheese

¼ cup butter

# Gnocchi à la Romaine

In a 2-quart saucepan bring milk, butter, salt, pepper, and nutmeg to a simmer. ♦ Reduce heat to low. Pour in Cream of Wheat and whisk vigorously with a wooden spoon until smooth. Continue stirring until mixture begins to thicken. Continue to cook for 5 minutes, stirring constantly to prevent scorching. ♦ Preheat oven to 375°F. ♦ Remove pan from the heat and stir in beaten eggs and 1 cup of the Parmesan cheese. ♦ Spread mixture evenly onto a buttered 9- by 11-inch cookie sheet using a rubber spatula. Refrigerate until firm and completely cooled. ♦ With a round or oval cookie cutter, cut mixture into circles and arrange in a lightly oiled ovenware dish so that rows overlap neatly. Sprinkle with the remaining 1 cup of Parmesan cheese, and place a few thin pats of butter on top. Bake until golden brown and serve immediately.

*Gnocchi à la Romaine are usually used as a garnish for poultry dishes, veal scallops, or cutlets, and would be a replacement for potatoes.*

*Garnishes 6 entrées.*

**1 quart milk**

**1 4-ounce stick butter**

**1 tablespoon salt**

**1 teaspoon white pepper**

**¼ teaspoon nutmeg**

**8 ounces Cream of Wheat**

**2 beaten eggs**

**2 cups grated Parmesan cheese**

**Additional butter for top**

# Risotto Milanaise

*Rice Milanaise*

In a large, thick-bottomed skillet with a lid, melt butter over low heat. Add onion and sauté until lightly browned. Add rice and stir to mix with onion. Add saffron, salt, pepper, and chicken stock. ♦ Cover and simmer over low heat for 20 minutes or until liquid is absorbed by rice. Serve with grated Parmesan cheese sprinkled over the top.

*Serves 6.*

**2 tablespoons butter**

**1 medium onion, chopped**

**2 cups long-grain rice**

**1 pinch saffron (about 10 threads)**

**1½ teaspoons salt**

**½ teaspoon pepper**

**4 cups chicken stock**

**3 tablespoons grated Parmesan cheese**

# Sauces

*Muriel Combettes, Jean Paul's
oldest child, at 3 years.*

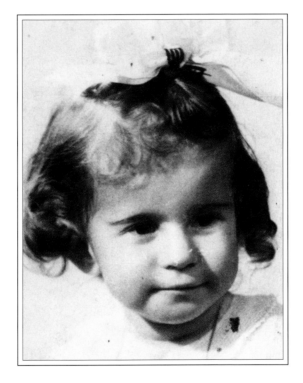

# Fonds Brun

*Brown Stock*

Place veal and beef in a lightly oiled roasting pan, and brown in a 425°F oven for 15 minutes, stirring occasionally to brown meat evenly. ♦ Add onions, celery, carrots, and leeks to roasting pan. Reduce oven temperature to 375°F, and return meat and vegetables to oven for 15 to 20 minutes, until vegetables are lightly browned. Stir occasionally. ♦ Transfer meat and vegetables to a large stockpot. Deglaze roasting pan with 1 quart of water and add to stockpot. Add more cold water until all ingredients are covered. Add salt, peppercorns, thyme, basil, and bay leaves and bring to a fast boil. Skim off foam and simmer for 3 hours. ♦ Strain through cheesecloth or a fine sieve and cool. Pour into containers and reserve.

*This recipe is used as a master base for Sauce Demi-Glace, Sauce Bordelaise, and Sauce Chasseur.*

*Yields 2 quarts.*

**3 pounds veal knuckle**

**3 pounds beef shin, cubed**

**2 large onions, coarsely chopped**

**3 ribs celery, coarsely chopped**

**3 medium carrots, coarsely chopped**

**2 leeks, coarsely chopped**

**1 gallon water (approximately)**

**1 tablespoon salt**

**1 tablespoon peppercorn**

**1 teaspoon thyme**

**1 tablespoon fresh basil or ½ tablespoon dried basil**

**3 bay leaves**

# FONDS BLANC

*White Stock*

In a large soup kettle, place the chicken, neck, and gizzard. Add water to cover. Bring to a boil, skimming off scum as it surfaces. Reduce heat and simmer for 15 minutes. ♦ Add remaining ingredients and cover, leaving lid slightly ajar. Continue simmering for 3 hours. ♦ Strain the stock through a strainer or a sieve lined with cheesecloth. Cool and refrigerate the stock for future use.

*White stock can be used in consommé, some chicken preparations, rice pilaf or risotto, Potatoes Boulangère, scallops, pannequets, Chicken Croquettes and, naturally, in many sauces.*

*Makes 3½ quarts.*

**1 5-pound hen or stewing chicken, including neck and gizzard**

**1 gallon cold water (approximately)**

**1 large onion, peeled and studded with 4 cloves**

**2 leeks (including green parts), coarsely chopped**

**2 large carrots, coarsely chopped**

**2 ribs celery with tops, coarsely chopped**

**1 pinch of thyme**

**1 bay leaf**

**1 teaspoon black peppercorns**

**2 tablespoons salt**

**1 tablespoon pepper**

# Sauce Béarnaise

*Béarnaise Sauce*

In a small saucepan place tarragon vinegar, white wine, salt, pepper, and shallots, and reduce over low heat to ⅓ cup. ♦ Transfer reduced liquid to a stainless steel bowl, gradually whisk in egg yolks, and place bowl in a pan containing 2 inches of simmering water. Place on low heat and whisk until mixture begins to thicken and turns light yellow. ♦ Remove from heat and gradually add clarified butter, whisking constantly. Add chopped parsley and tarragon.

*Yields 2 cups.*

⅓ cup tarragon vinegar

½ cup dry white wine

½ teaspoon salt

½ teaspoon white pepper

2 tablespoons shallots, minced

4 egg yolks, slightly beaten

8 ounces clarified butter

1 teaspoon chopped parsley

1 teaspoon chopped tarragon (dry or fresh)

# SAUCE BORDELAISE

*Bordelaise Sauce*

Place shallots and Burgundy in skillet. Bring to a boil over medium-high heat and reduce by half; add garlic. ♦ Stir in Sauce Demi-Glace, and simmer 5 to 10 minutes or until thick enough to coat meat or poultry. Serve immediately.

*Sauce Bordelaise is used as an accompaniment for broiled steaks and poultry. It is also used in Coq au Vin.*

*Yields 2 cups.*

**4 shallots, minced**

**1 cup red Burgundy**

**1 large clove garlic, minced**

**1 cup Sauce Demi-Glace
(see page 111)**

# Sauce Provençale

*Provençale Sauce*

Saute onions in olive oil until light brown. Add tomato purée, wine, thyme, basil, garlic, salt, and pepper. ♦ Stir over medium heat and simmer for 10 minutes.

*Use Sauce Provençale on Chicken Provençale, Codfish Provençale, red snapper, crayfish, or veal chops.*

*Yields 2 cups.*

**2 medium onions, diced**

**2 tablespoons olive oil**

**1 cup tomato purée**

**½ cup dry white wine**

**½ teaspoon dried thyme**

**1 teaspoon chopped fresh basil or ½ teaspoon dried basil**

**2 cloves garlic, crushed**

**1 teaspoon salt**

**½ teaspoon pepper**

# Sauce Béchamel

*Béchamel Sauce*

**M**elt butter in a heavy, thick-bottomed saucepan and add flour. Using a wire whisk, mix well, and stir in hot milk. Add salt and pepper and cook for 10 minutes over low heat, stirring often.

*This sauce is also used as a master base for Sauce Soubise and Sauce Mornay.*

*Yields 2 cups.*

½ cup butter

½ cup flour

2 cups hot milk

Salt and white pepper to taste

# Sauce Mornay

*Mornay Sauce*

Heat Sauce Béchamel in a bowl or saucepan over simmering water or in a bain-marie. Combine Gruyère and Parmesan cheeses. Gradually add to Béchamel, stirring constantly until well blended. Stir in butter.

*Sauce Mornay can be used to coat vegetables such as asparagus, artichoke hearts or bottoms, and cauliflower. It can also be used in some fish preparations, such as Fillets de Sole Clarence and Seafood au Gratin.*

*Yields 2 cups.*

**2 cups Sauce Béchamel (see page 107)**

**⅓ cup grated Gruyère cheese**

**⅓ cup grated Parmesan cheese**

**2 tablespoons butter, softened**

# Sauce Hollandaise

*Hollandaise Sauce*

*I*n a heatproof bowl place egg yolks, wine, lemon juice, water, salt, and pepper. ♦ Place bowl in a large sauté pan containing 2 inches of simmering water over low heat. Whisk yolks until they start to thicken and turn light yellow. ♦ Remove bowl from water bath and gradually add clarified butter, whisking constantly to form the emulsion. If sauce becomes too thick, add a few drops of warm water or lemon juice. Adjust seasoning and add cayenne.

**SAUCE MOUSSELINE (MOUSSELINE SAUCE):** is Sauce Hollandaise with whipped cream folded into it in the ratio of one part whipped cream to two parts Sauce Hollandaise. It is used to cover some dishes that are then set under the broiler or salamander, giving the sauce a warm, golden brown appearance.

*This French sauce was originally called Sauce Isigny, after a town in Normandy where the butters are of superior quality. During World War I, dairy products from Normandy were scarce. Butters from Holland, particularly those from Leyden, were more available and were imported into other countries; thus Sauce Isigny became Sauce Hollandaise. Chef Escoffier at the London Carleton adopted this name for the butter-based sauce in his* Guide Culinaire. *Hollandaise is also used as a master sauce for Sauce Mousseline and Sauce Béarnaise.*

*Yields 2 cups.*

**4 egg yolks**

**3 tablespoons dry white wine**

**1 tablespoon lemon juice**

**2 tablespoons water**

**½ teaspoon salt**

**½ teaspoon white pepper**

**1 pound butter, clarified**

**Dash cayenne**

# SAUCE CHASSEUR

*Mushroom Sauce*

Melt butter in a skillet over medium heat. Add mushrooms and shallots and sauté 2 minutes or until mushrooms are tender. ♦ Add Chablis, tomato purée, and Sauce Demi-Glace. Mix well, simmer for 2 minutes, and serve.

*Sauce Chasseur can be used in Chicken Sauté or as an accompaniment for squab, Cornish hen, roast beef, veal, scallops, and roast pork.*

*Yields 2 cups.*

**3 tablespoons butter**

**1 cup mushrooms, sliced**

**4 shallots, minced**

**½ cup Chablis**

**3 tablespoons tomato purée**

**1 cup Sauce Demi-Glace (see page 111)**

# Sauce Demi-Glace

*Demi-Glace Sauce*

Heat oil in a saucepan over medium heat. Add flour and stir with a wire whisk over low heat until mixture is smooth and turns light brown (this is called a "brown roux"). ◆ Slowly add brown stock to the roux while whisking over low heat until well mixed. Add tomato purée, salt, and pepper and simmer for 30 minutes.

*Yields 1 quart.*

**4 tablespoons cooking oil**

**4 tablespoons flour**

**1 quart Fonds Brun (brown stock, see page 102)**

**⅔ cup tomato purée**

**Salt and pepper to taste**

# SAUCE SOUBISE

*Soubise Sauce*

Melt butter in a saucepan and add onion. Cook over very low heat, covered, and stir frequently without letting onion brown. ♦ Stir in Sauce Béchamel and add nutmeg, tasting for seasoning. Cook another 5 minutes over very low heat. Purée by pressing through a sieve, if desired.

*Sauce Soubise can be used with hard-cooked eggs for a brunch buffet, to cover poached eggs for breakfast or brunch, to fill artichoke bottoms, as a garnish for vegetables, or on top of some types of quiche.*

*Yields 2 cups.*

**⅓ cup butter**

**2 cups minced onion**

**2 cups Béchamel Sauce (see page 107)**

**⅓ teaspoon nutmeg**

# Sauce Tomate Fraîche

*Fresh Tomato Sauce*

Simmer tomatoes in olive oil over low heat for a few minutes; add garlic, salt, pepper, and basil. Cook approximately 10 minutes until mixture is thick and smooth. Stir often to prevent scorching.

*Yields 2 cups.*

**2 cups fresh plum tomatoes, peeled, seeded and chopped**

**3 tablespoons olive oil**

**2 cloves garlic, crushed**

**1 teaspoon salt**

**½ teaspoon pepper**

**1 teaspoon chopped fresh basil or ½ teaspoon dried basil**

# Aïoli

*Garlic Dressing or Dip*

Place garlic in a bowl. Stir in mayonnaise and blend well. Add lemon juice and blend again. Refrigerate for up to 5 days in an airtight container.

*Yields 1¼ cups.*

**5 cloves garlic, finely minced**

**1¼ cups mayonnaise**

**2 tablespoons lemon juice**

# SAUCE AU ROQUEFORT

*Roquefort Dressing*

Place Roquefort cheese, pepper, and mayonnaise in a medium-sized mixing bowl and whisk together. ♦ Combine sour cream, lemon juice, olive oil, and Worcestershire sauce in a separate bowl and mix thoroughly. Gradually combine Roquefort/mayonnaise mixture with sour cream mixture, whisking vigorously until well blended. Refrigerate in airtight container up to 5 days.

*Yields 2 cups.*

½ cup crumbled Roquefort cheese

1 teaspoon white pepper

½ cup mayonnaise

½ cup sour cream

2 tablespoons lemon juice

½ cup olive oil

1 teaspoon Worcestershire sauce

# Sauce Mayonnaise

*Mayonnaise*

Combine egg yolks, mustard, salt, pepper, vinegar, and ¼ cup of the oil in the container of an electric blender or food processor. Cover and blend on low speed for 10 seconds. ♦ Remove cover, set blender to medium speed, and immediately pour in the remaining oil in a steady stream. Blend at high speed for 5 seconds. Transfer to an airtight container and use within 5 days.

*Yields 1¼ cups.*

**2 egg yolks**

**½ teaspoon dry mustard**

**1 teaspoon salt**

**½ teaspoon pepper**

**2 tablespoons white wine vinegar**

**1 cup salad or olive oil, divided**

# Jean Paul Vinaigrette Dressing

*I*n a mixing bowl combine all ingredients except olive oil. Mix well with a wire whisk. ♦ Add olive oil gradually, whisking constantly until combined. ♦ Cover and refrigerate until ready to use. ♦ Allow 2 tablespoons of dressing per serving for most recipes.

*Makes 4 cups.*

¼ cup Dijon mustard

¾ cup red wine vinegar

2 teaspoons salt

1 teaspoon ground black pepper

1 teaspoon tarragon

1 teaspoon chopped basil

6 cloves garlic, minced

2½ cups olive oil

# Desserts

*The Combette's 25th wedding anniversary,
1973, at the Sahara Hotel and Casino,
Lake Tahoe, Nevada.*

# ANANAS ANTILLAISE

*Pineapple Antillaise*

Slice off pineapple skin and remove all of the eyes. Slice crosswise into ½-inch slices, removing the core in the center of each slice. Marinate in rum for about 1 hour in refrigerator. ♦ Make a purée with the bananas. Whip cream with confectioners' sugar and vanilla; fold whipped cream into the banana purée. ♦ Divide pineapple slices among six individual serving dishes. With a pastry bag fitted with a fluted tube, pipe a mound of banana whipped cream on top. Sprinkle with chocolate sprinkles and chill in refrigerator for about 30 minutes before serving.

*Pineapples from Martinique are some of the best in the world, known for their juicy sweetness. This simple island recipe originates from the old French colony, and this is its first appearance in cookbook form.*

*Serves 6.*

**1 fresh, ripe pineapple**

**½ cup rum**

**3 bananas**

**⅔ cup heavy cream**

**½ cup confectioners' sugar**

**½ teaspoon pure vanilla**

**2 tablespoons chocolate sprinkles**

# Crème Caramel

*Cream Caramel*

Put sugar and water in a thick-bottomed saucepan. Place over medium heat and bring to a boil. Boil slowly until amber. Remove immediately from heat and pour into the bottom of a 10-inch oval ovenproof mold. Swirl around to evenly coat bottom of mold, and set aside. ♦ Preheat oven to 350°F. ♦ Pour milk and vanilla into a separate saucepan and heat until scalding. In a mixing bowl combine eggs and egg yolks with sugar. Whisk together until mixture turns pale yellow. Gradually pour in scalding milk while continuing to whisk. ♦ Pour custard into mold and place mold in a water bath so that one-fourth of the mold is immersed in water. Bake 45 to 60 minutes. The custard is done when a skewer inserted in the middle comes out dry. Remove mold from oven and allow it to cool slightly, then refrigerate until completely cool. ♦ To unmold, take a thin-bladed knife and, keeping the blade against the inside of the mold, cut all the way around the outer edge. Place a serving plate on top of the mold and turn over. If the custard does not drop down, tap the bottom of the mold to encourage it. ♦ This preparation may also be made in six individual molds.

*Serves 6.*

⅔ cup sugar

⅔ cup water

3 cups milk

1 teaspoon vanilla

5 whole eggs

2 egg yolks

⅔ cup sugar

# BISCUIT DE SAVOIE

*Savoie Cake*

Preheat oven to 350°F. ♦ Whisk together egg yolks, vanilla, and sugar in a mixing bowl. When yolks turn pale yellow, mix in flour and cornstarch. ♦ Whip egg whites in a mixing bowl until semi-stiff peaks form without reaching a dry stage. Carefully fold egg whites into yolk mixture until well combined. ♦ Pour batter into a 1-quart charlotte mold that has been buttered on the bottom and sprinkled with flour and a bit of sugar. Place cake on center rack of oven and bake for 30 minutes. The cake is done when it springs back to the touch. Remove cake from oven and let it cool. To unmold, take a thin-bladed knife and, keeping the blade against the inside of the mold, cut all the way around the edges. Place a serving plate on top of the cake and turn over. If cake does not drop free, gently shake the mold over the plate. Cool, wrap in plastic wrap, and place in refrigerator. ♦ Biscuit de Savoie can be used in Charlotte Savoisienne or in Trifle. It can also be used as a base for fruits with Crème Sabayon.

*Serves 8.*

**7 eggs, separated**

**1 teaspoon vanilla**

**1 cup sugar**

**¾ cup flour**

**¼ cup cornstarch**

**1 tablespoon butter**

**1 tablespoon flour**

**1 teaspoon sugar**

# CHARLOTTE SAVOISIENNE

*Charlotte Savoie*

Marinate candied fruits in kirsch for 1 hour. Whip cream with an electric mixer on high speed until it starts to thicken. Add vanilla, then gradually pour in sugar. Whip until stiff peaks form. Fold in candied fruit. ♦ Place the Biscuit de Savoie on a serving dish. Spoon whipped cream mixture into center of cake and serve. ♦ Optional: The recipe for Crème Sabayon on page 124 may be doubled and spooned over top of this dish before serving.

*Serves 8.*

**1 cup mixed candied fruits**

**2 teaspoons kirsch**

**1 cup heavy cream**

**1 teaspoon vanilla**

**¾ cup sugar**

**1 Biscuit de Savoie (see page 121)**

**Crème Sabayon (optional)**

# Mousse au Chocolat

*Chocolate Mousse*

Melt the chocolate over low heat in a heavy-bottomed saucepan or in a *bain-marie*. Mix in the strong coffee mixture and keep warm. ◆ In a medium-sized mixing bowl, whisk together egg yolks and sugar until they are slightly thickened and turn light yellow. ◆ Place bowl over a pan of simmering water. Continue to whisk eggs until a thickened ribbon stage is achieved. Add rum, if desired, and continue mixing for 1 more minute. ◆ Remove mixture from simmering water and, using a rubber spatula, fold in chocolate-coffee mixture. ◆ Immediately place bowl in refrigerator or in an ice-water bath. Stir occasionally until completely cool. ◆ In a separate bowl, beat egg whites until they form soft peaks. Fold into cooled chocolate mixture. Pour mousse into serving molds and refrigerate for 3 hours. ◆ Optional: Whip heavy cream with confectioners' sugar and coffee liqueur until stiff. Use as a garnish by spooning or piping on top of mousse.

*Serves 6.*

**8 ounces semisweet chocolate, cut into small chunks**

**4 tablespoons instant coffee, dissolved in 4 tablespoons water**

**5 eggs, separated**

**⅓ cup superfine sugar**

**3 tablespoons rum (optional)**

**TOPPING (OPTIONAL):**

**½ cup heavy cream**

**1 tablespoon confectioners' sugar**

**2 teaspoons coffee liqueur**

# CRÈME SABAYON

*Cream Sabayon*

lace all ingredients in a stainless steel bowl and whisk vigorously for about 1 minute. Place bowl in a skillet containing 1 inch of simmering water. Continue to whisk mixture constantly until sauce achieves a ribbon consistency. ♦ Remove bowl from simmering water and continue whisking for another 2 minutes or until sauce is lukewarm. Sabayon may be used as a sauce for many desserts or may be served alone, presented in a Champagne glass, either warm or cold. If the Sabayon is to be served alone, you may fold in the whipped cream to lighten the sauce.

*Serves 2 as a dessert or 6 as a dessert sauce.*

*3 egg yolks*

*3 tablespoons sugar*

*2 tablespoons sherry, Triple Sec, Curaçao, sweet Champagne or Muscatel*

*½ cup heavy cream, whipped (optional)*

# BANANES FLAMBÉES AU SABAYON

*Bananas Flamed With Cream Sabayon*

Peel bananas and cut in half lengthwise. Dredge in flour, dip in beaten egg, and dredge in flour again. ♦ Heat clarified butter in a skillet over medium-high heat. Sauté bananas in butter until each side is lightly browned and crisp. Remove bananas carefully from skillet and place in a heated chafing dish. Sprinkle with powdered sugar; pour rum or kirsch over bananas and set aflame. Ladle Crème Sabayon over bananas and serve.

*Serves 2.*

**2 bananas**

**1 egg, beaten**

**4 tablespoons clarified butter**

**2 tablespoons powdered sugar**

**1 tablespoon rum or kirsch**

**4 tablespoons all-purpose flour**

**Crème Sabayon (see page 124)**

# TRIFLE

**A**rrange the cake slices in a deep glass dish. Pour brandy and sherry over the top and allow it to soak in. Spread the jam over the top, then spoon a thick pastry cream over the jam and cake slices. Whip cream with vanilla and add sugar when cream begins to stiffen. Pipe a border around the dish. Sprinkle with toasted almonds and serve.

*Serves 4.*

**CRÈME PÂTISSIÈRE (THICK PASTRY CREAM):** Heat milk in a saucepan until scalding. In a stainless steel bowl, whisk together egg yolks, sugar, and vanilla for approximately 2 minutes or until mixture turns very light yellow in color. Gradually whisk in the scalding milk. Place mixing bowl over a pan containing 2 inches of simmering water. Continue to whisk the cream constantly until it begins to thicken. To cool rapidly, place the bowl in an ice-water bath and, using a ladle, roll the cream for 10 minutes until it cools to room temperature.

4 slices angel food cake or Biscuit de Savoie (see page 121)

¼ cup brandy

¼ cup sherry

4 tablespoons raspberry jam

¾ cup heavy cream

½ teaspoon vanilla

1 tablespoon sugar

½ cup sliced almonds, toasted

Crème Pâtissière (see below)


**CRÈME PÂTISSIÈRE:**

1 cup milk

3 egg yolks

⅓ cup sugar

½ teaspoon vanilla

# Melon au Frontignan

Cut a plug in the cantaloupe large enough to scoop out the seeds and threads, and pulp with a serving spoon. Reserve the plug. ♦ Scoop out the pulp and cut into chunks no larger than ½ inch. Place in a bowl, sprinkle with sugar, and stir until evenly coated. Add wine and continue stirring until mixed. ♦ Refill the hollowed melon with the pulp mixture. Replace the plug, set melon upright in refrigerator, and chill 1 to 2 hours before serving. ♦ Serve in hollowed melon rind presented on a serving bowl.

*The melon, though Asiatic in origin, was first introduced to France in 1533 by Catherine de Medici, wife of King Henry II of France, who was also responsible for bringing the French the fork. Melon is usually served either as an hors d'oeuvre or as dessert. There are many different species of melon, the French Cavaillon, or cantaloupe, being one of the best known.*

*Serves 2.*

**2½ to 3 pounds very ripe cantaloupe**

**⅓ cup sugar**

**½ cup Frontignan Muscatel or cream sherry**

# TARTE AUX POMMES

*Apple Tart*

Sift flour onto a pastry board and make a well in the center. Mix in butter, shortening, egg yolk, and salt. Work well with your fingertips and then add half of the water and continue working the dough. Gradually add more water as needed. ♦ Sprinkle flour over board to prevent dough from sticking. Knead the dough with the heels of your hands until ingredients are well mixed. Shape into a ball, place in a glass mixing bowl, and cover with a tea towel. Refrigerate for at least 30 minutes. ♦ Preheat oven to 400°F. ♦ On a lightly floured board, roll dough out to ⅛-inch thickness and carefully place in a 9-inch pie pan. Flute the dough around the edge of the pan. Arrange sliced apples neatly in the pan, starting from the outside edge and overlapping the slices, working toward the center. Sprinkle sugar and cinnamon evenly over apples. Place thin slices of butter on top. ♦ Place tart on bottom rack of oven and bake for 20 minutes or until edges of pastry are slightly browned. ♦ While tart is baking, mix together apricot jam and Cognac or brandy in a bowl until well combined. Remove tart from oven and allow it to cool slightly. Spread jam mixture over tart. Allow to cool completely before cutting and serving.

*Yields 1 9-inch tart.*

**2 cups flour**

**4 tablespoons sweet butter**

**2 tablespoons vegetable shortening**

**1 egg yolk**

**½ teaspoon salt**

**6 tablespoons cold water**

**1 to 2 medium-sized apples, peeled, cored, and thinly sliced**

**3 tablespoons sugar**

**1 teaspoon cinnamon**

**2 tablespoons butter**

**¾ cup apricot jam**

**3 tablespoons Cognac or brandy**

# Gâteau de Fruits au Rhum

*Rum Fruit Cake*

In a large bowl combine the first nine ingredients. Add 5 tablespoons flour and toss to mix well. Set aside. ♦ Preheat oven to 300°F. ♦ Butter a 10 × 4 × 3-inch loaf pan and line bottom and sides with buttered brown paper (use ¼ cup). ♦ In a large bowl, beat with an electric mixer at low speed 1 cup of butter and the sugar until light and fluffy; beat in eggs one at a time. ♦ Sift together 1½ cups of flour, baking powder, and salt. Stir in butter-sugar-egg mixture. ♦ Fold in fruit mixture. Stir in rum. ♦ Turn batter into prepared loaf pan and bake for 1¾ hours. Test doneness by inserting a skewer in the center of the cake; it should come out dry. Let cool in pan, then turn out on rack. ♦ To glaze the top, combine confectioners' sugar and lemon juice. Mix well and spoon over cake.

*Jean Paul obtained this recipe while in Brighton, England, in 1936, from an employee of a minister of the Church of England. It was later one of Dean Martin's favorites at the Sahara.*

*Serves 10 to 12.*

1 cup diced candied pineapple

1 cup white raisins

1 cup candied cherries

½ cup currants

3 tablespoons chopped candied lemon peel

3 tablespoons chopped candied orange peel

½ cup coarsely chopped almonds

½ cup coarsely chopped walnuts

½ cup chopped angelica

5 tablespoons flour

1¼ cups softened butter, divided

1 cup granulated sugar

3 eggs

1½ cups flour

1 teaspoon double-acting baking powder

1 teaspoon salt

¼ cup rum

1 cup confectioners' sugar

3 tablespoons lemon juice

# BAKED ALASKA

Arrange slices of cake (Biscuit de Savoie) in the bottom of an ovenproof dish and soak with Triple Sec. Place scoops of ice cream on top of cake and place dish in freezer. ♦ Place egg whites in a clean bowl and, using the wire mixing blades of an electric mixer, start beating at a slow speed. Gradually increase speed until egg whites begin to thicken and form a meringue. Gradually add 1 cup of the sugar to the egg whites and continue to whip until the meringue forms stiff peaks. Place meringue in a pastry bag with a #7 star tip. Remove dish from freezer and pipe meringue over the ice cream, covering it completely. (You may place the dish back in the freezer until ready to serve.) ♦ Sprinkle the remaining ½ cup of sugar over the top. Place the dish under broiler for 15 seconds or until top turns light brown. Heat brandy in a microwave oven until hot. Bring the dish to the table, pour the brandy over the dish, and flame. Cut and serve.

*Serves 2.*

**4 to 6 slices Biscuit de Savoie (see page 121), approximately 1 inch thick**

**3 tablespoons Triple Sec**

**2 scoops chocolate ice cream**

**2 scoops vanilla ice cream**

**4 egg whites**

**1½ cups sugar, divided**

**2 ounces brandy**

# New York Style Cheesecake

*P*reheat oven to 350°F. ♦ Mix graham cracker crumbs with melted butter and 1 tablespoon of the lemon juice. Lightly butter a 12-inch springform pan and press the graham cracker crumbs over the bottom and halfway up the sides to form the crust. Set aside. ♦ In a small mixing bowl, mix eggs and sugar together until combined, but don't whisk the mixture or air will be incorporated, making the cake dry. In a separate small bowl, mix the sour cream, lemon rind, and the remaining 2 teaspoons lemon juice and set aside. ♦ In a medium mixing bowl, soften cream cheese by mixing with a wooden spoon or spatula. ♦ Very gradually add egg mixture to cream cheese, making sure that you scrape the sides of the bowl. Do not allow lumps to form. When egg mixture is well combined with cream cheese, mix in the sour cream and lemon mixture using the same procedure to prevent lumps. ♦ Pour mixture into the crust-lined pan and bake until filling sets, approximately 1 hour. Check doneness by shaking pan slightly. The mixture should move in a solid mass. Remove from oven and allow to cool completely. ♦ Place raspberry preserves in a pastry bag with a #2 plain tip and pipe a border of preserves around outer edge of cheesecake. Decorate with fresh raspberries if desired. Cut and serve.

*Serves 12 to 16.*

**2 cups graham cracker crumbs**

**2 tablespoons melted butter**

**1 tablespoon plus 2 teaspoons lemon juice**

**4 eggs**

**1 cup sugar**

**2½ cups sour cream**

**Grated rind of 1 lemon**

**2 cups cream cheese, softened at room temperature for 1 to 2 hours**

**¾ cup raspberry preserves**

**Fresh raspberries (optional)**

# Vanilla Ice Cream

*H*eat milk with the vanilla bean or vanilla extract in a medium saucepan until scalding; remove from heat. In a stainless steel mixing bowl combine egg yolks and sugar with a whisk and beat until mixture turns light yellow in color. ♦ If a bean was used for vanilla flavoring, remove it from the heated milk. Gradually pour milk into egg and sugar mixture, whisking constantly. Place bowl over simmering water and continue to whisk gently until custard begins to thicken. Remove from heat and continue to stir until mixture cools slightly. Place bowl in refrigerator until it cools completely. ♦ Process the mixture in an ice-cream maker. When mixture starts to thicken, add cream and continue processing until a soft ice cream texture is achieved. Remove and serve, or store, covered, in the freezer for later use.

*Yields 6 cups.*

**1 quart milk**

**1 vanilla bean or 1 teaspoon vanilla extract**

**8 egg yolks**

**1 cup sugar**

**½ cup heavy cream**

# WINES FOR COOKING

### White Wines

White wines for cooking should be dry and heavy in alcohol. Chablis made from the Chardonnay grape is the most popular wine, but a good substitute is white vermouth, excellent for oven-poaching fish such as sole, halibut, and salmon or shellfish such as mussels, clams, and oysters.

Chablis is also used in braising, sautéing, sauces, and so on.

### Red Wines

Red wines such as Burgundy, a full-bodied wine, when used in beef or Chicken Burgundy Style or sauces such as Bordelaise, must be reduced to remove the raw flavor of the wine. They are also used in marinades.

### Madeira and Port Wines

These are the final flavoring for sauces. In the United States, sherry is the most popular substitute for Madeira or port wines.

### Cognac

Cognac is the most widely used in French cooking, from sauces to desserts, for flaming seafood or Crêpes Suzette. Brandy is the substitute for Cognac.

### Grand Marnier, Curaçao, Cointreau

Orange liqueurs are used most specifically as flavoring in flaming desserts, to marinate fruits and to flavor custards, sabayon, and creams.

### Muscatel

Muscatels, such as Frontignan (probably the most famous), are excellent for melons and sabayons.

Each course in a ceremonial dinner has a specific and traditional wine for nearly every course, chosen to enhance each particular dish.

Dry Sherry is traditionally served with hors d'oeuvres or soup.

First Course (escargots, scampi, foie gras, smoked salmon, terrines, quiches, prosciutto, crudités): Dry white wines such as Chablis, Macon Blanc, dry Sautérne. American counterparts would be a California Chablis or a Washington Riesling.

Fish and Shellfish: Medium-dry white wines such as Sancerre Moselle Le Bishop, White Burgundy, or Pinot d'Alsace. American counterparts would be a Washington or California Chenin Blanc or Riesling.

Meat Entrées, Roasts: Red Bordeaux or Burgundy, Chambertin or Chateauneuf du Pape. American counterparts would include Cabernet Sauvignon, Merlot, Pinot Noir.

Poultry: Any wine — rosé, red, or white. A special mention for Cabernet Sauvignon (Napa Valley).

Dessert (Crêpes Suzette, Baked Alaska, creams and custards): Champagne, Asti Spumante, or sweet Vouvray.

# Buffet

Serving a buffet is the answer to feeding a crowd in a limited space. It also permits the host or hostess to enjoy the company of his or her guests and relax with them.

A buffet means that you arrange your dishes on your dining table or kitchen counter so that your guests may help themselves while you continue to share their company. If it is a formal reception, the buffet is set in the dining room with a beautiful tablecloth in white, red, or gold; candlesticks in crystal; and a centerpiece of fruits or flowers according to the season. On a side table arrange the silver, plates, glasses, and napkins. The living-room cocktail table may be used. But for your family, you serve the buffet on the kitchen counter. The items that should be served include salads; roasted meat or stew; vegetables; pasta, rice, or potatoes; and dessert.

# Buffet Menu I

Salmon Cured in Olive Oil

Salade de Haricots Verts

French rolls

Suggested wine: Chardonnay

*The Cured Salmon may be eaten as it is, served on toasted bread (white, wheat, or pumpernickel), or may be lightly broiled over coals or grilled and served with lemon wedges. This is a gourmet appetizer to be served in a buffet, at poolside, or as an hors d'oeuvre.*

# Buffet Menu II

Salmon à la Norvégienne

Salade de Pommes de Terre Nîmoise

Oeufs à la Chimay

Tomates Antiboise

Fresh rolls and butter

Suggested wine: Chardonnay or Sancerre

# Buffet Menu III

Langouste à la Albert

Croquettes de Volaille

Moules Marinière

Filet de Sole Clarence

Moules Mayonnaise

Aubergines à la Provençale

Suggested wine: Sancerre

# Index